Praise For
Your Book or Your Excuse

Alinka has coached hundreds of bestselling authors, and it shows. She doesn't preach; she teaches. This book reframed my thinking: authority isn't what you earn at the end of your career; it's what you build with your words right now.

**Javier Cavada Camino, PhD (Dr. Eng.) |
President and CEO, Mitsubishi Power EMEA and
USA National Bestselling Author**

What makes this book stand out is how practical it is. It's equal parts business strategy and personal challenge. Alinka doesn't just tell you that publishing builds credibility; she proves it through real leaders who used their books to open doors, shape industries, and leave legacies. The narrative here subtly persuades; the benefits to you individually in becoming an author are vast and varied – the process is significant and as these voices agree, it is well worth the journey.

**Karen Chetwynd |
CEO, Montessori Global Education**

Your Book or Your Excuse isn't just a book about writing, it's a call to lead. Alinka Rutkowska challenges readers to stop waiting for the "right time" and start defining their legacy now. Through compelling stories, research, and lived experience, she proves that authorship is leadership in action. By the final page, I wasn't thinking about someday, I was outlining the book that will shape my next decade.

**Carl Grant III |
Author, *How to Live the Abundant Life***

Your Book or Your Excuse feels like a conversation with a mentor who refuses to let you play small. Alinka's track record of hundreds of leaders, multiple bestsellers, and global reach gives her advice undeniable weight. But it's her tone that makes the difference: encouraging yet uncompromising. You finish this book ready to lead, not just read.

**Dan Williams |
CEO, ONELIFE Senior Living**

There's a quiet confidence in these pages that stays with you. Alinka doesn't hype you up; she holds you accountable. Her message is simple but profound: leaders who publish lead longer. Reading this made me realize I've been hiding behind busyness when what I needed was courage.

**Tamara Nall |
CEO & Founder, The Leading Niche**

This book made me stop scrolling and start creating. It's not just for writers, it's for anyone who wants to turn experience into impact. Alinka shows how a single book can become your most powerful business tool, your best sales asset, and your clearest legacy. It's bold, wise, and deeply practical.

**Alex Melen |
Co-Founder, SmartSites**

Alinka Rutkowska and Leaders Brands have redefined what it means to publish with purpose. Their approach goes far beyond writing, it's about positioning, visibility, and legacy. The book made me realize that true leadership isn't about waiting to be discovered; it's about partnering with people who know how to make your story unforgettable.

Keri Jaehnig |
Founder & CEO, Idea Girl Media

Alinka's words are a mirror. You'll either see your excuses clearly or your next big opportunity. Either way, you won't walk away unchanged.

Matthew J Hall |
CEO and Inventor, Toilet Accessories Llc.

For those seeking to understand the "Why" and the commitment, you can't unread this. Once you see what Alinka reveals about the 1%, you'll never see leadership or excuses the same way.

Thierry Nguyen |
Biopharma Professional, Founder,
Bodhi Nature LLC

This book reminded me why I wrote mine — to ignite that spark in others. It's not just about writing; it's about finally doing the thing you've been putting off for far too long. Every page is a push toward action.

Kumar R. Parakala |
USA National Bestselling Author,
Lead to Disrupt **| CEO, Tabhi**

This isn't theory. It's proof that legacy doesn't happen by accident, it's built word by word.

Takis Athanassiou |
Business Consultant, Author, and Trainer

Reading this felt like pulling back the curtain on how real thought leaders are made. Alinka and her team at Leaders Brands have coached hundreds of authors, and you can feel that expertise in every example. They don't just publish books, they engineer platforms that open doors, land media features, and create lasting credibility. This is the playbook every serious leader should have.

Geoffrey M. Reid | Best-Selling Author, TEDx Speaker, Former Global CEO, Fractional CEO at geoffreymreid.com

Are you still thinking about your "someday" book? Imagine it as though you're at the gym trying to lift the "book" barbell. It's huge. It stares back. You consider faking a typing-finger cramp so you can go skip the workout. Then, Alinka and the Leaders Brands team show up like the world's nicest trainers: they set the weight just right, spot your reps, and even put the weights back when you're done. They don't preach - they stack your wisdom, plate by plate. Their method is the workout plan that trims excuses, builds mental muscle, and makes the heavy things feel doable. Your Book or Your Excuse is the sign above the squat rack: "Strong stories, stronger impact." With the right coaching, any leader can turn war stories into a powerful body of work that keeps flexing for years.

Fred K. Weigel, Ph.D. | Husband, Father, Lieutenant Colonel, USA (ret), Wallstreet Journal/USA Today Best-Selling Author

YOUR BOOK OR YOUR EXCUSE

WHY THE 1% OF LEADERS PUBLISH—AND
THE 99% GET FORGOTTEN

Alinka Rutkowska

Copyright © 2025 Alinka Rutkowska
Published in the United States by Leaders Press.
www.leaderspress.com

All rights reserved. No part of this book may be reproduced or transmitted in any form or by any means, electronic or mechanical, including photocopying, recording, or by any information storage and retrieval system, except by a reviewer who may quote brief passages in a review to be printed in a magazine or newspaper. The contents of this book may not be used to train large language models or other artificial intelligence products without written permission from the copyright holder.

All trademarks, service marks, trade names, product names, and logos appearing in this publication are the property of their respective owners.

ISBN 978-1-63735-404-9 (pbk)

ISBN 978-1-63735-403-2 (ebook)

Table of Contents

PART I: What Happens When You Lead with a Book 1

Chapter 1: Doers Lead. Dreamers Wait. Which Are You?..........5
    This Is Not Another "How to Write a Book" Manual......... 5
    Publishing Is About Leadership, Not Authorship 6
    Hobbyists Make Excuses. Leaders Make Books. 6

Chapter 2: The Hidden Cost of Not Publishing.....................9
    The Divide Between Hidden Experts and Recognized Leaders 9
    The Psychology of Authority....................................10
    Leaders Act. Hobbyists Wait.....................................11

Chapter 3: Someone's Book Is Generating Your Leads—Just Not Yours.. 13
    Why Books Create Shared Identity 13
    The Data: Books Outperform Other Content 14
    How Leaders Structure Books as Lead Engines..............14
    Why Articles and Posts Don't Compare 15
    The Risk of Staying Silent 16

Chapter 4: Lead Conversion—How Your Book Sells Before You Step In 19
    Why a Book Builds Instant Trust 19
    How Sales Cycles Shrink 20
    Why Books Raise Deal Size 21
    The Psychology of Feeling Known.............................21
    Real-World Proof...22

Your Book or Your Excuse

Chapter 5: Opening Doors—How Books Go
Where You Can't...25
    Why Books Travel Further than You..............................25
    The Power of Tangibility 25
    The DHL Story...26
    Why Books Secure Introductions 26
    Books Open Policy Conversations 27
    The Missed Opportunity 27

Chapter 6: Winning Media—How Books Put You
in the Spotlight...29
    Why Media Chases Authors 29
    Books Create the "Interview Effect" 30
    Real-World Examples...30
    The Opportunity You're Missing 31

Chapter 7: Leaving a Legacy—How Your Book Lives On 33
    Why Your Book Becomes Your Legacy..........................33
    The Names Everyone Knows 34
    A Legacy That Lives Beyond You...................................36

PART II: Proof in Action—Leaders Who Published to Lead 37

Chapter 8: Po Chung, the Co-Founder of DHL....................39
    Facing the Blank Page 40
    Why the Book Matters...41
    The Impact on Readers 42
    What He Gained, What He Avoided 43
    A Legacy That Endures..44

Chapter 9: Javier Cavada Camino, CEO of Mitsubishi
Power EMEA..45
    Shifting the Mindset 45
    The Turning Point..46

    A Legacy of Speed and Simplicity 47

Chapter 10: Karen Chetwynd, CEO of Montessori
Global Education 49
    Overcoming Fear Through Reflection 50
    Choosing the Partnership 50
    A Different Future Without It 51
    Looking Ahead 52

Chapter 11: Chris Tufton, Former Minister of
Health and Wellness 55
    The Problem He Couldn't Solve Without a Book 55
    Why He Wrote It 56
    The Beliefs He Had to Overcome 57
    What the Book Allowed Him to Do 57
    How It Impacted Readers 58
    The Feelings He No Longer Had to Live With 59
    A Conversation with the Future 59

Chapter 12: Mark Nureddine, Founder and CEO of
Bull Outdoor Products 61
    The Entrepreneur Who Never Thought
    He'd Be an Author 61
    The Turning Point 62
    The Process That Made the Book Possible 62
    Turning Business Challenges Into Lasting Influence 63
    The Response That Erased His Doubts 64
    The Transformation: From Doubt to Impact 65
    The Regret He Doesn't Have to Live With 65
    A Gift That Keeps on Giving 66

Chapter 13: Carl Grant III, CEO at Rainmakers Group 67
    The Book Inside 67

- Doors the Book Opened 68
- How the Book Impacted His Readers 69
- The What-If He Never Faced 69

Chapter 14: Tamara Nall, CEO at The Leading Niche 73
- Why a Book Was the Answer 73
- Making the Leap to Authorship 74
- The Breakthrough 74
- Impact on Readers 75
- The Ripple Effects 75
- The Burden Lifted 77

Chapter 15: Andy Allen, Founder of The 80 Percent Project ... 79
- The Challenge That Needed a Bigger Platform 79
- Why the Book Had to Be Written 80
- Breaking Through His Own Barriers 80
- The Doors the Book Opened 81
- Readers' Transformations 82
- No More What-Ifs 82

Chapter 16: Tom Fedro, Founder and CEO at Paragon Software Group 85
- What Training Alone Couldn't Do 85
- What Made the Difference 85
- The Mindset Shift 86
- What Became Possible 87
- What It Meant to Readers 87
- The Ripple Effect 88

Chapter 17: Alinka Rutkowska, Co-Founder of Leaders Brands 89
- Before the Book 89
- The Turning Point 90

The Book That Built My Future 92
The Truth That Changed Everything 93

PART III: Winners Find Ways, Losers Find Excuses 95
    Why 99 Percent Will Never Have a Book.....................96

Chapter 18: "I Don't Have Time" 97
    Leo Tolstoy: Making Writing a Habit 98
    The Prime Minister Who Made Time to Write 98
    Phil Knight: Building Nike *and* Writing **Shoe Dog**.........100

Chapter 19: "It's Too Expensive" 105
    Resourcefulness over Resources: The Jobs Lesson 105
    Howard Schultz: Refusing to Take "No" for an Answer ... 107
    Walt Disney: No Money, No Backing, No Excuses 109

Chapter 20: "I Need to Talk To…" 113
    Whose Responsibility Is It?.................................... 113
    Why Do You Need to Run It by Someone Else? 114
    Do You Want to Resent Your Partner? 115

Chapter 21: "I'll Publish After…" 117
    Tim Ferriss: From 26 Rejections to Global Authority.... 117
    Reid Hoffman: Don't Wait Until "After" 120
    Ben Horowitz: Why Would Anyone Care? 122

Chapter 22: "I Still Need to…" 127
    "I Still Need to Do More Research".......................... 127
    "I Need to Sleep on It" 129
    "I Need to Think About It".................................... 132

Chapter 23: The Real Excuse Behind Every Excuse............ 135

Your Book or Your Excuse

PART IV: Your Book, Without the Excuses 137

Chapter 24: Leaders Brands' Proven Process 139
    Strategic Positioning Comes First 139
    Why Positioning Matters 139
    Manuscript Development 140
    Editing and Quality Assurance 141
    Design and Layout 141
    Distribution 142
    Pre-Launch 142
    Launch 142
    Post-Launch 143

PART V: The Path Forward 145

Chapter 25: The Future Is Already Here 147

Chapter 26: The Call That Changes Everything 149

Sources 151
    Books and Reports Cited 151
    Reports, Studies, and Industry References 152
    Web and Reference Sources 153
    Media and Public Domain References 154

PART I

What Happens When You Lead with a Book

Your Book or Your Excuse

History is full of leaders who changed their industries, their cultures, even their countries. Yet most of them are forgotten. They led, they built, they influenced in their time, but their names disappeared with the next generation. A small fraction—the one percent—chose differently. They published. They captured their ideas in a book. And because of that, they are remembered not just for what they did, but for what they wrote.

Think about **Sun Tzu**. Little is known about him personally. Historians even debate whether he was a single figure or a composite of multiple strategists. Yet *The Art of War* has endured for over two thousand years. It is still studied in military academies, business schools, and boardrooms. Sun Tzu the man remains a mystery, but Sun Tzu the author is immortal.

Or consider **Niccolò Machiavelli**. He was neither a king nor a general. He held modest political roles in Florence, roles that might have faded into obscurity. Yet his book *The Prince* turned his name into an adjective. "Machiavellian" is now used globally to describe cunning, ruthless political strategy. Without the book, Machiavelli might have been a footnote. With it, his ideas continue to shape how leaders are described, half a millennium later.

Consider **Adam Smith**, a professor of moral philosophy who never ran a business, never held elected office, and never built an empire. Yet his 1776 masterpiece, *The Wealth of Nations,* became the foundation of modern economics. Politicians, investors, and business leaders still invoke his work today. Few can describe what he looked like or how he lived. But his book is the reason we remember him.

Mary Wollstonecraft lived in an era when women's voices were rarely recorded, let alone amplified. She had no formal power. Yet her book *A Vindication of the Rights of Woman* gave her a permanent place in history as one of the earliest advocates for gender equality. She is remembered because she wrote.

In the 20th century, **Dale Carnegie** transformed from a farm boy into a teacher of public speaking. He wasn't a head of state or a titan of industry, yet *How to Win Friends and Influence People* has influenced more leaders than most presidents or CEOs. The book has sold over 30 million copies and continues to shape the way professionals build relationships nearly a century later. Without that book, Carnegie's legacy would have remained part of the 99 percent—influential in his time, but forgotten by history.

Viktor Frankl was one of millions of Holocaust survivors. His personal story could have been lost in the enormity of history's tragedy. But by writing *Man's Search for Meaning*, he turned his suffering into a message that continues to inspire millions. His insights on resilience and purpose outlive him and give him a voice in every generation since.

And then there's **Stephen Covey**. Before his book, he was a consultant and professor. After *The 7 Habits of Highly Effective People*, he became one of the most recognized voices in leadership and personal development worldwide. His book didn't just sell—it created a movement. More than 40 million copies later, Covey's habits are still taught in boardrooms, classrooms, and coaching programs everywhere.

These names illustrate a truth leaders cannot afford to ignore. History has always rewarded those who record their lessons. From philosophers and generals to business thinkers and psychologists, the pattern is the same: success alone fades, but written ideas endure. People are not remembered simply because they were successful in their time. They are remembered because they turned their success, their thinking, and their philosophy into a book that could outlive them. The one percent of leaders who publish write their way into history. The 99 percent who don't are either forgotten—or worse, misrepresented by others who write the story and control the narrative.

CHAPTER 1

Doers Lead. Dreamers Wait. Which Are You?

What separates the one percent from the 99 percent? There are two types of business authors.

The first is the dreamer or hobbyist. Hobbyists tinker. They talk about writing "someday," download "how to write a book" manuals, attend free webinars, and try to DIY their way to credibility. Their book—if it ever gets finished—becomes a vanity project: something to check off a bucket list, impress family and friends, but never move markets or command authority.

Then there's the doer—the true leader. The leader doesn't dabble; they act decisively, hire professionals, and treat books not as projects, but as **strategic tools** that reinforce their authority. For them, a book isn't proof they can write. It's proof they can lead.

This Is Not Another "How to Write a Book" Manual

This book is not for hobbyists. If you're looking for tips on sentence structure, grammar hacks, or DIY formatting, you've come to the wrong place. Hundreds of books in the Authorship category already cover that.

But if you're a leader who understands that publishing is about **positioning, branding, and identity**, then you've made it to the right place. Leaders from DHL, Montessori, and Mitsubishi came here not just to publish books, but to **build legacy, credibility, and authority that lasts.**

Publishing Is About Leadership, Not Authorship

Because here's the truth: writing a book isn't about becoming an author. It's about becoming a better, more effective leader. It's about stepping into the identity of someone who doesn't just participate in conversations—but shapes them. Someone who doesn't just run a business—but leaves a mark on an industry. Someone who refuses to be forgotten.

Hobbyists Make Excuses. Leaders Make Books.

Throughout these pages, you'll see the difference between hobbyists and leaders. You'll see how leaders use books as **24/7 salespeople**, multiplying their authority and opening doors that would otherwise stay closed. You'll see how excuses like "I'm too busy" or "I'm not ready yet" aren't really about time or readiness at all: they're about who they are. They're the language of hobbyists—not leaders.

And you'll see how true leaders publish again and again, not because they need another book, but because they know authority isn't a one-time achievement. It's an ongoing identity.

Alinka Rutkowska

This book is your invitation to make a decision: stay a hobbyist, or step fully into the leader you were meant to be.

Leaders don't wait for someday. They decide, they act, and they publish now.

CHAPTER 2
The Hidden Cost of Not Publishing

Less than one percent of professionals who say they want to write a book actually follow through and publish. Surveys consistently show that around 80 percent of people dream of writing a book someday, yet only a fraction (less than one percent) ever act. If you publish, you don't just stand out; you immediately claim the authority that the silent majority forfeits by default.

The Divide Between Hidden Experts and Recognized Leaders

Publishing creates a visible divide. Without a book, no matter how skilled you are, you remain a hidden expert. With one, you elevate yourself into the public consciousness as a thought leader. But one book only gets you so far. One book might spark curiosity, but it rarely sustains authority. Each new book compounds your credibility until your position at the top is unquestionable.

Have you heard of James Kouzes and Barry Posner? In their landmark work on credibility, they show that leadership rests on two pillars: expertise and trustworthiness. Expertise answers the question, "Do you know what you're talking about?" Trustworthiness answers, "Will you stand behind it?" When you publish a book, you demonstrate both. Your book proves you have knowledge worth sharing and that you're confident enough to stake your reputation on it. That's why a book carries more weight than a LinkedIn post, a podcast interview, or even a keynote: it is a permanent symbol of your authority.

The Psychology of Authority

Psychologists talk about **authority bias**—the human tendency to grant more trust and be influenced by those who appear authoritative. A book is one of the strongest authority signals you can possess. Before someone even opens it, the fact that you *wrote* it positions you as an authority. You're no longer "one of many professionals." You're "the one who wrote the book."

Think about it. Notice how, even after reading just a few pages, your perception of me has shifted. Do you see me as just another voice in your field—or as the author whose words you're studying right now? That's the dividing line. Without a book, you're invisible. With a book, you're immediately set apart.

The real danger is underestimating the cost of not publishing. That cost is rarely obvious to you. **You don't see the client who signed with your competitor because their book built trust first**. You don't hear about the media opportunity they accepted because they had the credibility marker you lacked. You'll never know about the speaking engagement you weren't invited to because you didn't stand out. These are the silent losses of authority—the doors that close before you even knew they were there.

Leaders Act. Hobbyists Wait.

Yes, you already have some authority. But authority at the highest level isn't about what you've accomplished—it's about how you are positioned. If you tell yourself you'll "do it someday," you're still thinking like a hobbyist. If you decide to publish now, you're acting like a leader. You don't publish because you're ready. You publish because you know that **acting like the authority you want to be is how you become it.**

The authority gap will always exist. Which side are you on? Will you stay the hidden expert—respected by a few but overlooked by most—or will you publish, claim your authority, and step into the identity of the leader you know you're meant to be?

CHAPTER 3
Someone's Book Is Generating Your Leads—Just Not Yours

One of the most obvious signs of a true leader is that they have followers. The highest-quality followers are often attracted through a book you wrote. Think about it: books don't just offer ideas—they bring people into your circle.

Why Books Create Shared Identity

Researchers in social identity and leadership, including Alexander Haslam, highlight that effective leaders don't simply "lead by doing." They shape how others see themselves and the group they're part of. Leadership often involves creating a strong social identity—a shared vision that followers adopt. A book carries this power: it gives your future readers a lens through which to see themselves—as aligned with your ideas, dreams, and leadership.

When you publish, you're not just giving information—you're cultivating a collective identity. And that's how followers show up, even before they meet you. That's why many thought leaders report that readers naturally become subscribers, clients, or collaborators simply because the book invited them into the same mindset.

The Data: Books Outperform Other Content

Start with the data. *According to NetLine's 2024 State of B2B Content Consumption Report* (NetLine, 2024), **ebooks are still the #1 format buyers seek out,** representing 39.5 percent of all content demand across 6.2M first-party registrations—and that demand grew 34.5 percent year over year. NetLine's 2024 analysis also ties content consumption to purchase intent, noting more than a third of professionals expect to make a purchase within 12 months of engaging, with certain formats signaling even stronger intent. If you don't have a substantive, book-length asset in their path, you're simply not in the queue when they're shortlisting suppliers.

Decision-makers also trust thought leadership more than marketing—and act on it. Edelman and LinkedIn's *2024 B2B Thought Leadership Impact Study*—summarized by Ragan Communications and Curzon PR—found that more than 3,500 decision-makers, nearly three-quarters view thought leadership as a more trustworthy basis than product collateral. Additionally, 75 percent say high-quality thought leadership prompted them to research a product or service they hadn't previously considered. In other words, the right book doesn't just attract attention—it creates demand from buyers who weren't even in the market.

How Leaders Structure Books as Lead Engines

Now look at how top operators openly structure their books as lead engines:

As **Alex Hormozi** explains in *$100M Leads* (2023), he gives his books away free or at cost "in hopes of earning your trust," and pairs each launch with bonus assets and a content hub that routes readers into his ecosystem. He says the point is getting strangers to raise their hands—leads first, sales later. This is the modern "authority-to-inbound" flywheel in action.

Donald Miller's StoryBrand framework anchors an entire training business on the back of his books (*Building a StoryBrand*, *Marketing Made Simple*). From the book, readers are channeled to sold-out StoryBrand workshops, certifications, and coaching—a clear evidence trail that the book isn't the product; the relationship is. **If your book never invites the reader into a next step, you're doing free public education for your competitors.**

Chris Voss's *Never Split the Difference* shows the enterprise version of the same model: book → corporate training → courses "beyond the book." Even if you sell to boards and Fortune 500s, the book is the front door to your high-trust, high-ticket services.

Notice what all of these have in common: they offer architecture around the book—landing pages, value add-ons, invitations to the next step. The content is generous, but the path is deliberate.

Why Articles and Posts Don't Compare

If you're thinking, *"But we already publish articles and social posts,"* consider how buyers actually behave. NetLine's data shows long-form content captures the most demand—ebooks dominate downloads and signal active problem-solving. At the same time, Edelman and LinkedIn's research shows thought leadership is the "de-risking layer" that gets unfamiliar buyers to engage, even among the 95 percent of the category who aren't "in-market" right now. Quality thought leadership seeds the 95 percent with future intent. A book is your most credible, portable form of that thought leadership.

Here's a quick gut check: are you using your book the way a leader would, or are you just dabbling? Leaders don't stop at "I have a book." They make sure it actually works for them.

A book done right earns permission. It positions you as someone worth listening to and creates trust before you ever enter the room.

It also collects raised hands. Smart leaders include simple next steps—maybe a bonus chapter, a worksheet, or an audio guide—so readers have a way to stay connected.

From there, the book qualifies interest. People who want more will follow the trail to a workshop, a consultation, or a discovery call.

And over time, every copy out in the world becomes a billboard—on desks, in boardrooms, at events—quietly reminding people of who the authority is.

That's the difference. Hobbyists hope their book gets noticed. Leaders design theirs to work like a system, bringing the right people closer every day.

The Risk of Staying Silent

If you don't give your market a book-length asset to request, pass around, and act on, you're gifting the demand to whoever does. That's the uncomfortable reality: when a buyer starts their self-directed research—which is how most B2B journeys now begin—they'll find someone's book, just not yours. And the author they read first is the one they'll research, shortlist, and trust.

Make this tangible. Imagine a CFO forwards a dog-eared chapter to the CEO with a note: *"Worth a look."* That moment is the pipeline forming without you in the room. If your competitor's book is what's circulating, you're not losing deals at the proposal stage; you're losing them months earlier, at the moment of curiosity.

The fix isn't more posts. It's a book engineered for lead gen: a clear point of view, outcomes your market cares about, and explicit next steps baked into the reading experience (bonus chapter downloads, a diagnostic link, a private roundtable invite). That's how you convert anonymous readers into known contacts, and known contacts into qualified opportunities—at scale, 24/7.

When the market goes looking for answers, the author gets the call. If that author isn't you, you're financing your competitor's pipeline.

If you want to be unavoidable in your space, act accordingly: ship the book, wire the funnel, and let the pages start prospecting.

CHAPTER 4

Lead Conversion—How Your Book Sells Before You Step In

You've seen it before: some people walk into a meeting already trusted and taken seriously. Others spend the first half-hour scrambling to prove themselves. The difference? **Credibility.**

A book is one of the fastest ways to pre-sell your credibility before you ever enter the room.

Why a Book Builds Instant Trust

Have you heard of **Amy Cuddy's Harvard research on first impressions**? Popularized by *Wired*, she found that when we meet someone, we instantly judge two things: "Can I trust them?" and "Can they do the job?"—which she calls trustworthiness and competence. A book delivers both at scale, and without you saying a word.

Think about **the Elaboration Likelihood Model (ELM)** developed by psychologists Richard Petty and John Cacioppo, a classic in persuasion theory. It says people are more likely to be influenced by messages that they've thought about or processed more deeply. Long-form content like a book is one of those high-impact, high-attention channels that moves someone from passive to deeply engaged far more reliably than a tweet or an email ever could.

And behavioral psychologist **Robert Cialdini**, in his classic *Influence*, calls this the **authority principle**. People are more likely to trust and follow those who demonstrate expertise in visible, public ways. A book is one of the strongest "authority cues" you can own.

Need more? In manufacturing, a 2025 report by RH Blake—featured in *Manufacturing Tomorrow*—showed that **thought leadership shortens long B2B sales cycles**, because it aligns with buyers' need for credibility and quick confidence in complex decisions. *Forbes* has also emphasized that thought leadership "reduces perceived risk," making buyers more receptive even in volatile markets.

How Sales Cycles Shrink

In modern B2B, Gartner and McKinsey research shows that **buyers complete more than 70 percent of their decision-making before ever talking to a sales rep**. That means most of the selling happens in private—through the research buyers do on their own time. If your book is in their hands during that window, you're not just part of the research process—**you're shaping it.**

This is why conversations feel so different when prospects have read my books. When someone comes to me after reading *How I Sold 80,000 Books*, *Outsource Your Book*, or *Your Book or Your Excuse*, the dynamic shifts immediately. They're warmer. They don't ask vague questions like, *"So what do you do?"* They arrive informed, educated, and often halfway to the decision already. The calls are sharper, the conversations more intelligent, and often, the sale is essentially done before we even start.

That's the power of shortening the sales cycle. Your book does the heavy lifting before you even enter the room.

So ask yourself: would you rather keep repeating the same surface-level conversations with people who don't get it yet... or would you rather have prospects show up already convinced, already trusting you, and basically saying, "Just tell me where to sign"?

Why Books Raise Deal Size

It isn't just about speed—it's also about value. ***Harvard Business Review*** has shown that when buyers perceive a provider as a thought leader, they're willing to pay a premium. Why? Because thought leadership reduces perceived risk. People don't mind paying more for someone they already trust.

In fact, one *Forbes* analysis during economic downturns found that **companies producing thought leadership were less likely to face pricing pressure**—buyers felt safer betting bigger on them. Your book puts you in that premium category. It flips the question from "Why are you expensive?" to "How do I get access to you?"

The Psychology of Feeling Known

There's another layer: **psychological safety.** A book creates what I call asynchronous intimacy—the kind that happens when readers spend hours with your voice on their own time. By the time they finally talk to you, they already feel like they know you. This "I feel like I know you" effect accelerates trust in ways no pitch deck ever can.

That intimacy shortens the gap between stranger and client. It's not persuasion anymore. It's confirmation. And the proof is everywhere you look.

Real-World Proof

This isn't just theory. The most successful leaders use books exactly this way—as trust-building engines that warm up audiences, shorten the path to yes, and open doors they never could have forced open on their own.

Take **Michael Hyatt**. When he published *Platform: Get Noticed in a Noisy World*, he wasn't just trying to add "author" to his résumé. He engineered the book as a front-end trust builder for his larger coaching and training programs. The book positioned him as the go-to voice for leaders trying to stand out online. Readers didn't just buy the book—they wanted the system behind it. As a result, his workshops and courses filled up with pre-sold attendees who already believed in his method. That single book laid the foundation for his eight-figure business, because every reader arrived "warm" before he ever met them.

Or look at **Simon Sinek**. Before *Start With Why*, he was an insightful consultant with a handful of corporate clients. After the book, he became the philosopher of modern leadership. *Start With Why* didn't just sell copies; it reframed how entire companies thought about purpose. By the time Sinek walked into boardrooms at Fortune 500 companies, he wasn't pitching—he was confirming. Executives had already read his ideas, bought into his philosophy, and were eager to pay him to help them implement it. His book pre-sold him into keynote slots, corporate consulting retainers, and even advisory roles with governments and the military.

Then there's **Brené Brown**. Her book *Daring Greatly* wasn't positioned as a how-to manual; it was a manifesto on vulnerability and courage in leadership. That book didn't just sell—it became a cultural touchstone. Leaders at companies like Google and Microsoft, as well as high-ranking officials in the US military, started quoting her work. By the time she walked into those organizations, she didn't need to prove herself. Her book had already done the work, creating trust at scale. The intimacy of her writing made readers feel like they knew her personally. That emotional connection translated directly into doors opening at the highest levels of business and government.

The pattern is undeniable: Hyatt, Sinek, and Brown didn't write their books as end products. They built **pre-sell assets** that turned readers into buyers, companies into clients, and entire industries into amplifiers of their ideas. The books carried the credibility for them, allowing the authors to skip the cold-start conversations and step straight into trust, authority, and opportunity.

So for you... do you want to walk into meetings like Hyatt, Sinek, or Brown—already trusted and pre-sold—or keep wasting half your calls convincing prospects you're credible?

CHAPTER 5
Opening Doors—How Books Go Where You Can't

A book has a passport you don't. It circulates freely in boardrooms, lands on desks you'll never sit at, and sparks conversations you'll never overhear. It can secure introductions and influence policy discussions that your emails will never reach.

Why Books Travel Further than You

Think about how executives actually make decisions. According to McKinsey's 2023 B2B research, corporate purchasing decisions now involve an average of **six to ten stakeholders** across a company. Emails and sales pitches rarely reach all of them. But a book? It gets passed around. It becomes the document everyone refers back to in the room when you're not there.

This is how authority multiplies. You're not just one voice on a call. Your book sits in the middle of the table, literally or figuratively, and speaks for you in the conversations you can't attend.

The Power of Tangibility

There's a reason physical books open more doors than digital brochures. A 2017 study in the *Journal of Consumer Research* shows that **tangible objects create stronger memory and trust associations** than digital ones. When a prospect holds your book, flips its pages, and highlights a passage, they've already invested in your thinking in a way a PDF never could. That tactile connection translates into deeper trust and stronger recall—the two currencies you need most when you're not in the room.

The DHL Story

One of the clearest examples of this power came from Po Chung, co-founder of DHL. He didn't find us through LinkedIn like so many of our other clients. He found us through my book *Outsource Your Book*. He bought it himself, gave it a number in his personal bookshelf catalog, and filed it there alongside the other important titles in his collection.

Think about that for a moment. Here was a leader with layers of gatekeepers, the kind of person most people would never be able to reach directly. **Yet he was the one who reached out to us.** Why? Because he read a book that spoke to him, trusted the authority behind it, and decided he wanted the same results for himself. That book opened a door that cold emails, LinkedIn messages, or sales calls never could have breached.

Why Books Secure Introductions

Networking works best when someone else vouches for you. A book acts as that vouch. When an executive hands your book to a colleague and says, *"You should read this,"* they've just introduced you with more weight than any cold outreach ever could.

According to Edelman and LinkedIn's *B2B Thought Leadership Impact Study*, **89 percent of decision-makers said high-quality thought leadership improved their perception of a brand**, and **49 percent said it directly influenced them to award business**. A book is simply thought leadership at its highest proof point. It's the introduction that travels for you.

Books Open Policy Conversations

At the highest levels of influence—industry groups, think tanks, even governments—books shape conversations in ways that PowerPoints and emails can't. Policymakers and influencers may never respond to your pitch, but they'll read and cite a book.

That's exactly what Po Chung, co-founder of DHL, did. He used his own book to ensure his ideas about leadership and organizational culture entered the policy dialogue around the world. His words traveled further than he could—shaping decisions long after the meetings ended.

The Missed Opportunity

Now ask yourself: when was the last time your email was forwarded from a manager to a CEO, printed out, and debated around a table? Rarely, if ever. But books get passed along. They get quoted. They get recommended.

That's the risk of not having one: you're invisible in the rooms where decisions get made. Someone's ideas will be in that discussion. The only question is—will they be yours?

Your Book or Your Excuse

A book is more than a calling card. It's an authority multiplier that travels without you, speaks when you're not present, and makes introductions you could never engineer yourself. Leaders don't wait for introductions—they let their books walk into rooms for them.

The choice is simple: you can keep hoping your pitch emails get forwarded… or you can put your book in circulation and let it start conversations you can't.

CHAPTER 6
Winning Media—How Books Put You in the Spotlight

When was the last time a journalist emailed you out of the blue for a quote? Or a podcast host reached out to book you as a guest? If it hasn't happened yet, here's why: you don't have the most powerful media credibility marker there is—a book.

Why Media Chases Authors

Reporters and producers live by one rule: *get credible sources fast*. According to a Pew Research Center survey, nearly **nine in ten journalists say speed and credibility are the top pressures in their work**. They don't have time to chase down every consultant or executive, so they go to the experts who already look like authorities—and the fastest way to signal authority is to be an author.

Public relations studies show that **being quoted in media increases trustworthiness and brand recognition.** But journalists are selective about who they feature. They look for people with proof points: previous coverage, visible expertise, or most often, a published book. A book isn't just content; it's shorthand for "this person has done the work and can be trusted."

Books Create the "Interview Effect"

Podcasters, YouTubers, and radio hosts all want guests who can carry a conversation. A book solves that problem instantly. It gives them a ready-made script: *"Tell us about your book."* That's why you'll notice the overwhelming majority of business podcast guests are authors. The book guarantees substance.

For you, the book does double duty. It not only gets you booked, but it also makes the interview itself easier. Instead of selling yourself, you're discussing ideas you've already laid out, with the authority of someone who literally *wrote the book* on the topic.

Real-World Examples

Adam Grant. Before *Give and Take*, Adam Grant was a respected Wharton professor known mainly in academic circles. Publishing vaulted him into the media mainstream. Outlets like *The New York Times*, *TED*, and *Fortune* suddenly had a fresh, credible voice to quote on leadership and workplace behavior. Today, Grant is one of the most cited business thinkers in the world, hosting his own podcast *WorkLife*—all because a book signaled he was media-ready.

Cal Newport. Newport had been writing on productivity and computer science for years, but it was *Deep Work* that turned him into a go-to expert. After its release, he was invited to write op-eds for *The New York Times* and *The Wall Street Journal*, became a regular guest on top podcasts, and even gave a widely shared TED Talk. His book didn't just sell—it gave journalists confidence that there was an authoritative voice worth broadcasting to millions.

Eric Ries. Ries had credibility in Silicon Valley, but *The Lean Startup* exploded his visibility. Media outlets like *Harvard Business Review*, *The Economist*, and *Fast Company* latched onto his framework. Suddenly Ries wasn't just another founder—he was a spokesperson for an entire movement. His book opened doors to venture capital firms, government innovation programs, and global conferences.

Chris Voss. Former FBI negotiator Chris Voss had an impressive résumé, but it was his book *Never Split the Difference* that made him a media fixture. The book gave journalists and podcast hosts a reason to feature him—a compelling story plus packaged insights. It wasn't long before he became a household name on shows like *MasterClass* and top-tier business podcasts, something that would never have happened if his expertise stayed locked in his career bio.

Sophia Amoruso. Known initially for founding *Nasty Gal*, it was her book *#GIRLBOSS* that transformed her into a cultural icon and a media magnet. The book sparked a Netflix series, a podcast, and countless media profiles. Journalists didn't just write about her company—they wrote about *her ideas*, because the book gave them a clear narrative hook.

The Opportunity You're Missing

Without a book, media outlets may never even consider you—no matter how qualified you are. You simply don't register on their radar. But the moment you put a book into the world, the dynamic flips. Suddenly you're not the one chasing attention. You're the one being invited.

Your Book or Your Excuse

So the question becomes simple: do you want to keep competing for attention one pitch at a time, or do you want your book to do the pitching for you—twenty-four hours a day, to every journalist, podcaster, and event organizer looking for the next authority in your field?

CHAPTER 7
Leaving a Legacy—How Your Book Lives On

Do you want to focus only on this quarter's results, or are you the kind of leader who thinks long term, even generations ahead?

If you're reading this, I'm guessing it's the latter. You already know leadership isn't just about today's wins. It's about the impact that outlasts you, the conversations that continue after you've left the room, and the reputation people whisper when you're not around.

That's what a legacy is, and here's the truth: **you don't stumble into one. You build it intentionally.**

Why Your Book Becomes Your Legacy

Researchers studying leadership and legacy have uncovered something important: legacy isn't just what you've done—it's the story people tell about you afterward. A study published in the *Journal of Management & Organization* found that leadership transforms into legacy when it becomes part of a narrative—something others continue to share and pass on. That's exactly what your book does. It traps your story and your way of seeing the world in a form people can revisit, share, and build on.

Think about it: tweets vanish in moments, conference talks fade in hours, speeches go stale fast. A book, though? A book lives. It sits on desks, ends up in libraries, gets passed to interns. Your philosophy gets bottled up, stashed on shelves, and carried into classrooms. It becomes a reference point long after you've delivered the ideas in person—and maybe even longer after you're gone.

The Names Everyone Knows

Are you familiar with names like **Peter Drucker, Jim Collins, Stephen Covey, Clayton Christensen, Daniel Kahneman, Sheryl Sandberg, and Howard Schultz**? Of course you are. And it's not just because of their companies or careers. You know them because they invested in leaving a legacy—and they did it through books.

Peter Drucker is still called the "father of modern management," even though he passed away nearly two decades ago. Why? Because books like *The Effective Executive* and *Management: Tasks, Responsibilities, Practices* are still studied in MBA programs and cited in boardrooms. Drucker didn't just manage companies; he left a blueprint for how leaders still manage today.

Jim Collins carved out his legacy with *Good to Great* and *Built to Last*. His concepts—from the "Hedgehog Principle" to "Level 5 Leadership"—continue to guide annual strategy sessions and executive retreats worldwide. His frameworks became shorthand in business conversations, ensuring his ideas outlive him.

Stephen Covey's *The 7 Habits of Highly Effective People* is one of the most influential leadership books ever written, with over 40 million copies sold. It's been a permanent fixture on recommended reading lists for CEOs, executives, and coaches for more than three decades. Covey passed in 2012, but his habits are still being taught to the next generation of leaders.

Clayton Christensen reshaped innovation itself with *The Innovator's Dilemma*, introducing the concept of *disruptive innovation*, and with it, a framework that technology companies, venture capitalists, and even policymakers still rely on. Though he passed in 2020, the term he coined is still used daily in conversations about the future of business.

Daniel Kahneman, Nobel laureate and psychologist, changed how leaders understand decision-making with *Thinking, Fast and Slow*. The book became required reading in management, investing, and product development. Even after his passing in 2024, his ideas about cognitive bias and judgment errors continue to shape business and economics.

Sheryl Sandberg's *Lean In* wasn't just a bestseller—it was the spark for a global movement on gender equity in the workplace. The book gave leaders a new vocabulary to discuss opportunity, ambition, and organizational culture, ensuring Sandberg's legacy stretches far beyond her years at Facebook.

Howard Schultz documented his comeback story in *Onward: How Starbucks Fought for Its Life Without Losing Its Soul*. The book gave entrepreneurs and executives a timeless playbook on protecting and reviving a brand's identity during crisis. Schultz's leadership story became bigger than Starbucks itself because he captured it in writing.

A Legacy That Lives Beyond You

I saw this firsthand with **Po Chung, the co-founder of DHL**. We worked with him on what became his final book, written explicitly for legacy. Po has since passed away, but he was deeply happy with the mark he left behind. He told me how proud he was of that book, how much it meant to him to have his ideas captured for future generations. I am honored that I could help him create it. His story proves the point: a book is more than words on paper. It's a legacy preserved.

There's also powerful, albeit indirect, research that shows just how lasting the impact of books really is. A 2016 study by researchers at Yale University, published in *Social Science & Medicine,* looked at more than 3,600 adults and found that people who read books regularly—just a few hours a week—lived nearly **two years longer** than non-readers, even after accounting for health, wealth, and education.

So yes, you could almost say that by publishing your book, you're not only building your authority and leaving your legacy—**you're actually contributing to prolonging your readers' lives by two years.** Talk about impact!

PART II

Proof in Action—Leaders Who Published to Lead

Your Book or Your Excuse

You've seen how books build authority, open doors, generate and convert them into clients, win media, and leave a legacy. You've also seen how leaders like Drucker, Covey, and Christensen shaped entire industries through the words they left behind. And you've heard how Po Chung, co-founder of DHL, used his final book to secure the legacy he wanted.

Let me introduce you to just a few of the 500+ leaders we've helped become authors—leaders you can meet directly as a client. You'll see the challenges they were facing before their book, and the transformations that followed once their book was out in the world.

These aren't abstract success stories. They're real accounts of leaders who used their books to open doors to boardrooms, attract high-value clients, secure speaking engagements, and build legacies that will outlast them. As you read, picture yourself in their place, because the same results are possible for you.

CHAPTER 8
Po Chung, the Co-Founder of DHL

When you meet Po Chung, there's a calm clarity—he doesn't rush his words. He paints pictures with them. And in many ways, that's not surprising—he's not only the co-founder of DHL International, one of the most successful global service companies in history, but also an accomplished painter. Yet when Po decided to write his book *Designed to Win*, it wasn't just to retell DHL's meteoric rise. It was because there was a problem he and his colleagues couldn't solve by simply doing more of what they'd always done.

The problem was this: DHL had grown into a global phenomenon almost by instinct. Decisions were decentralized. Culture was "caught, not taught." Mistakes were celebrated as lessons. But when Po stepped back decades later, he realized much of what they had built risked being lost to time. Younger leaders, eager entrepreneurs, and even DHL's new generation of employees didn't have access to the thinking that had guided DHL's improbable journey from a scrappy start-up to a network spanning over 220 countries. Without a map, the essence would fade.

"We never doubted we would succeed," Po wrote, "but we didn't talk about our realization process because we thought everyone instinctively knew what we knew. Later, we discovered they didn't."

That was the book-shaped hole in front of him. Without codifying the DHL way, the essence of the company's leadership philosophy—the human values, the stories, the hard-earned lessons—would vanish or be misunderstood. And beyond DHL, there were thousands of new entrepreneurs hungry to globalize but with no map. *Designed to Win* would be that map.

Facing the Blank Page

When Po Chung set out to write *Designed to Win*, it wasn't with the intention of crafting a personal memoir. It was about putting into words what had guided DHL from its earliest days—insights that had often gone unspoken.

He admitted that, in the 1970s and 80s, DHL's leaders didn't think to articulate what made the company successful. *"We thought everyone had the same instinct we had,"* he later reflected. When they discovered that wasn't true, their way of working became something of a guarded secret. It wasn't until decades later, with the benefit of hindsight, that Po felt the need to define and share the core of DHL's leadership philosophy.

And yet, writing wasn't his natural medium. "I write slow, I think fast," he said with a smile. He realized he needed someone who could keep up with the pace of his ideas, someone to capture them as he spoke. He had tried co-authoring before, but it took too long. When he discovered that we could help him shape a book in three months, he didn't hesitate. "If you don't really love doing something, you probably won't do a good job," he explained. And he didn't love solitary writing—but he did love talking, discussing, and teaching.

Writing the book meant revisiting mistakes as well as victories. He was clear that DHL's formula for success didn't appear fully formed—"it took nearly twenty years before we collectively figured it out." Documenting that process required candor, but it also created an opportunity: to pass on a roadmap so future leaders could build global networks without repeating the same missteps.

For Po, putting pen to paper wasn't about doubt— it was about responsibility. Silence would have meant letting those lessons fade. Writing meant ensuring they would endure.

Why the Book Matters

For Po, *Designed to Win* wasn't just about telling stories of bungee-jumping in New Zealand with colleagues or recounting how DHL legally fought for the right to exist in Hong Kong. It was about crystallizing what had always been intuitive: that leadership in a service economy cannot be about control, but about cultivating competence, character, and care.

The book gave him the framework to articulate what DHL had embodied but never named. It transformed oral traditions and scattered anecdotes into principles future leaders could apply. And in doing so, it preserved DHL's legacy as more than a logistics company—it became, in Po's words, a "purpose brand," a network where values became a religion.

Writing also allowed him to bridge East and West, showing how Asian philosophies like *chi* (energy) informed DHL's culture just as much as Western management theory did.

That blend was part of DHL's secret sauce, and now it had a permanent home in print.

The Impact on Readers

Readers responded with enthusiasm.

Ken Allen, then CEO of DHL eCommerce Solutions, said the book was "essential reading for today's entrepreneurs"—a blueprint for building an enduring legacy without being swept away by management fads.

Victor Fung, one of Asia's most respected business leaders, praised it as "five books in one," calling it indispensable for anyone seeking to understand the convergence of Asian and Western business models.

James Thompson, founder of Crown Worldwide, went further: "Rarely do readers get the opportunity to read about the creation of a global industry from the people that made it happen. This belongs in every business school library in the world."

Beyond endorsements, Po was quietly moved by how the book found its place. It appeared in media outlets and was displayed alongside books by Nobel Prize winners and World Economic Forum speakers. Asked how that felt, he simply replied: "I feel humbled."

For young entrepreneurs, the book validated their desire to think globally, not just nationally. For DHL employees, it became a touchstone of identity—proof that what they lived every day was part of a bigger philosophy. And for executives outside the logistics world, it was a window into how values, not just systems, build truly global organizations.

What He Gained, What He Avoided

By writing the book, Po allowed himself to live without the gnawing regret of unshared wisdom. He didn't want to be one of those leaders whose lessons evaporated once the boardroom door closed.

He often reminded his peers of the importance of recording their journeys: "There are two ways you can have your name remembered. One is sponsoring a building at a university, the other is writing books. Writing books is a lot less expensive than leaving a building."

Instead, he knew he had captured something timeless. His readers would carry the DHL way into industries far beyond logistics—education, healthcare, social enterprise. His family, too, could point to the book as a record of what he had stood for.

The feeling Po avoided was silence. **Silence that comes when leaders pass away without passing on their philosophy.** Silence that leaves the next generation reinventing the wheel instead of standing on the shoulders of giants.

By putting DHL's story into words, Po not only celebrated the company's triumphs but also made peace with its struggles, its mistakes, and its improbable victories. The book became his way of saying: *We were here. We built something that lasts. And here's how you can, too.*

A Legacy That Endures

And that's why *Designed to Win* matters. It isn't just a chronicle of DHL's rise—it's Po sharing the lessons of a lifetime, as if he were across the table from you, saying: *"This is how we did it, and this is how you can apply it too."*

Though Po Chung has passed on, his voice continues to live through his book—and even in these pages. His insights, his values, and his way of thinking are preserved here, offering guidance to every reader who picks up the story. In that sense, **he didn't just design DHL to win; by writing *Designed to Win*, he designed his wisdom to endure**, carrying his legacy forward long after him.

CHAPTER 9
Javier Cavada Camino, CEO of Mitsubishi Power EMEA

When I first met Javier Cavada Camino, I could sense the speed of his mind. He spoke with urgency, but not recklessness—each word carried weight, each phrase distilled from decades of leadership across continents. He didn't need jargon. He had lived it.

And yet, for years, Javier carried inside him the raw material for a book he never wrote. His career spanned Bosch, Wärtsilä, Mitsubishi, and more. He had led teams in Europe, China, the Middle East, and Africa. He had wrestled with outdated factories, reorganized global businesses, and stood in the middle of transformations that changed industries. But a single thought kept gnawing at him:

"Isn't this already out there? Haven't Toyota, Amazon, or Steve Jobs already said it all?"

That belief nearly silenced him.

Shifting the Mindset

What changed everything was a realization: **principles don't transform people—stories do.**

Readers don't just want to be told about speed; they want to feel what it was like when a 25-year-old Spaniard was thrown into a failing foundry and had to win over managers twice his age. They don't just want a lecture on simplicity; they want to see what it meant when four sprawling divisions were collapsed into two, when silos came crashing down and teams rediscovered purpose.

And no case study could replace the lived experience of being sent to China in 2008—discovering that what looked like a growth mission was in fact a near-crisis: broken supply chains, technical failures, and the closure of European factories whose operations had to be transplanted halfway across the globe.

It was there that Javier forged his motto: **speed and simplicity**. He saw how bureaucracy and fear kept organizations running like mice on a wheel—lots of motion, no progress. And he learned that real leadership was about clarity, persistence, and adaptability in the storm.

These weren't abstract principles. They were scars and triumphs etched into his story.

The Turning Point

Javier admits that without putting his story into writing, something would have remained unfinished. "Every achievement," he reflects, "becomes the basement for the next one. **Success is not the end—it's always the next summit.**"

By contributing his chapter to *Success DNA*, he confronted the limiting belief that his insights were redundant. They weren't. They were necessary—because no one else could tell them through his eyes.

A Legacy of Speed and Simplicity

Now, Javier is working on his own book. The lessons that once threatened to remain scattered—in memories, in boardrooms, in factories—are being shaped into a legacy.

He tells his daughter three things he hopes she carries for life: never let anyone limit you, trust yourself and those who believe in you, and choose the right partner. Those lessons are not just for her—they're for every reader who will one day hold his book.

What could have been lost—the doubts, the near-failures, the moments of persistence—are now becoming part of a written record. **Instead of silence, there will be stories. Instead of regret, there will be a roadmap.**

That is why Javier is writing today. Not to add another title to his career, but to ensure his wisdom endures. To prove, in his own words, that speed and simplicity are not just corporate mantras but lived truths. And to remind us all, **the summit you reach today is only the base of the one you climb tomorrow.**

CHAPTER 10
Karen Chetwynd, CEO of Montessori Global Education

When I first met Karen Chetwynd, I was struck by her blend of warmth and steel. As the CEO of Montessori Global Education, she carried both the weight of a century-old philosophy and the urgency of bringing it alive for a modern world. There was nothing casual about her mission. Every sentence she spoke carried an undertone of responsibility: to the children, to the parents, to the educators, and to the generations yet to come.

Her presence was that of someone who knows exactly why she has taken her place at the table—and who will not easily be moved from it.

Karen's book, *Led by the Child*, was born out of this deep sense of purpose. For her and her team, the manuscript was not simply a collection of chapters; it was a culmination of years of reflection on where Montessori Global Education must stand today.

Her children grace the front cover, a deliberate choice. "They are the center of what matters for me," Karen said. "I want to share that expression with all our readers." It is a reminder that behind all the debates on curriculum, policy, and regulation, the child remains the heart. **To be led by the child, in her eyes, is not a slogan but a responsibility.**

Overcoming Fear Through Reflection

Yet the path to publication was not without hesitation. Montessori already occupies an honored space in academic literature. Did the world really need another book on the subject?

Karen's answer was yes—but with a crucial distinction. Much of the existing work was written for scholars, not for parents beginning their journey or for educators seeking practical, modern context. She wanted to offer "fresh eyes." But with freshness came risk. Would a new approach land as intended, or be dismissed as dilution?

The doubt was real.

Karen admits she never fully silenced the fear of judgment. But through the writing process, she discovered something greater: clarity. "There comes a point at which the clarity of the message is more important than anything else," she reflected.

Writing became a mirror. It forced her and her team to distill their mission into what she now calls their "non-negotiables." What they would not compromise. What they would stand for, regardless of external pressure. Montessori herself taught the value of reflection, and in Karen's process, reflection became the antidote to fear.

Choosing the Partnership

When asked why she partnered with us, Karen had one word: trust. From our earliest conversations, she recalls feeling a confidence that the book would be achievable and that it would reach broad audiences.

While many consultants push leaders to narrow their message, Karen resisted. Parents, teachers, grandparents, policymakers—all are part of the Montessori ecosystem. To her, segmenting them felt artificial; she wanted a book that spoke to them all, and she felt assured we could help her achieve it.

When the book was complete, something shifted. Karen describes it as a new firmness in her conversations. No longer willing to bend to shifting agendas, she held her ground with partners. "We are very clear," she told me. "We know what we want the landscape to look like. We don't have time for everything. We must be dedicated to what we do, for the benefit of children."

The book had crystallized her non-negotiables. And once written down, deviation was no longer possible.

Karen calls *Led by the Child* a springboard. In the short term, it consolidates conversations and lends credibility to partnerships. In the long term, it acts as a manifesto—a call to action that galvanizes a movement.

Montessori Global Education, as she sees it, is one of the gatekeepers of Maria Montessori's legacy. That role carries responsibility, but also an opportunity to ignite hearts and minds. A book, she realized, is more than information; it is a declaration of intent.

A Different Future Without It

When I asked her what life might look like if she had chosen *not* to write the book, Karen did not hesitate: "We'd still be languishing somewhere, trying to clarify our meaning."

Without the book, she believes the organization would still be caught in cycles of opportunism, chasing projects without strategic alignment. **The book gave the team a collective vision—something bigger than the CEO, something the entire organization could rally around.** "This is not about me," she insists. "This is about the team supporting a vision that made this possible."

The book has reshaped how others see Karen and how she sees herself. Trustees now speak of Vision 2040 and beyond. Where once Montessori Global Education thought in three-to-five-year plans, the horizon has expanded to decades.

The book made that possible. It announced to the world that this was not an organization chasing trends, but one committed for the long haul.

Looking Ahead

Ultimately, Karen frames her legacy through a powerful metaphor. Montessori Global Education, she says, is like the trunk of a tree—its roots run deep, anchoring in history and values, its branches are children, reaching outward into the future. The trunk's role is not to dictate where the branches grow but to give them strength, stability, and nourishment.

> "The greatest sign of success for a teacher is to be able to say, 'The children are now working as if I did not exist.'"
> —Maria Montessori

That is what it means to be *led by the child*: never to walk in front of them, but to support them so they can flourish.

Karen's journey is a reminder that **writing a book is not about ego. It's about responsibility. If you have a message that can change lives, you owe it to the world to put it into words.**

When I met Karen, I didn't just see a CEO. I saw a woman who had chosen courage over comfort, impact over silence. She could have kept her philosophy close, but instead she made it public. Because she did, classrooms are calmer, homes are happier, and children are being heard.

The question is: will you?

The world doesn't need another intention. It needs your book.

CHAPTER 11
Chris Tufton, Former Minister of Health and Wellness

When I first sat down with **Dr. Christopher Tufton**, I wasn't speaking with just another politician or public figure. I was talking to a man who had spent nearly a decade at the helm of Jamaica's Ministry of Health and Wellness—and who found himself, quite literally, "on the bridge" when COVID-19 struck. The weight of an entire nation's fears and hopes rested on his shoulders. And somewhere in the middle of managing that crisis, he decided he needed to write a book.

Why? Because Chris knew something that many leaders never quite accept: **moments of history fade fast**. The lessons slip away, the stories become distorted, and the raw humanity of the people who lived through them is lost. For him, the pandemic wasn't just a once-in-a-lifetime public health challenge. It was a human drama filled with mistakes, triumphs, grief, and resilience. He wanted to capture it before it disappeared.

The Problem He Couldn't Solve Without a Book

In those early days, Jamaica's first "patient zero" arrived from the UK, sparking fear across the island. Soon after, tragedies followed—like Jodi, a young mother who died from pregnancy complications after doctors wrongly suspected she had COVID. Chris carried these stories with him every day.

the minister who steered Jamaica through COVID, but as someone recognized **globally as a thought leader** on crisis management and health resilience.

The book became a launchpad. Invitations to speak, opportunities to mentor, and international recognition—all opened up because he had a tangible, structured story to share. No longer a fleeting voice in the news cycle, he became a **documented witness to history**.

And then there was **legacy**. Chris often uses that word. For him, the book is a way of leaving something behind—not just for his children or countrymen, but for the students of policy and public health who will inherit the world's next crisis.

How It Impacted Readers

Readers responded with heartfelt admiration. One described *Wild Flavours* as "a masterly paced thriller more than a political memoir"—an electrifyingly candid account of COVID-19 that proved "something beautiful can come from crisis." Another praised its focus on "transparency, trust, and decisive action," calling it a testament to leadership in turmoil.

Reviewers consistently highlighted its authenticity and compassion, noting how Tufton's candor gave voice to Jamaica's collective resilience. One wrote that the book was "a comprehensive, compelling account of Jamaica's fight against COVID-19"—rich with lessons for the next generation of leaders.

The Feelings He No Longer Had to Live With

Perhaps the greatest gift of the book was what it spared Chris from: **regret.**

Without it, he might have always wondered if the lessons of those years would fade, if his perspective would be lost in the noise of politics. By writing *Wild Flavours*, he ensured the experience was preserved authentically—not filtered through headlines or hindsight.

He didn't have to live with the nagging feeling of missed opportunity. Instead, he could look at the book and know: **the moment was captured, the legacy secured.**

A Conversation with the Future

When I asked Chris what advice he would give to someone considering writing a book, his response was simple: **"You just need to do it. The hardest part is to start."**

He acknowledges that the process might feel uncertain, that you may not know where it's heading. But conviction, once put into motion, has a way of carrying you through.

In the end, that's what his journey illustrates: a book isn't just about sharing expertise—it's about reflection, connection, and leaving something behind that outlives you.

For Chris Tufton, *Wild Flavours* was more than a memoir of a crisis. **It was a bridge between past and future, between personal experience and public good.**

Your Book or Your Excuse

And perhaps that's the lesson for every aspiring author: you're not just writing for yourself. You're writing so no one has to face the next storm without the light of the last one to guide them.

CHAPTER 12
Mark Nureddine, Founder and CEO of Bull Outdoor Products

The Entrepreneur Who Never Thought He'd Be an Author

I'll never forget the first time Mark Nureddine told me about his dream. For years, he had carried this idea: a book that would take all the lessons he had learned building Bull Outdoor Products—starting in a garage in 1992 and growing it into an international brand with over 900 dealers in 15 countries—and put them into the hands of entrepreneurs who desperately needed guidance. He'd watched so many small business owners struggle with avoidable mistakes, and he knew he had something valuable to give.

The problem? He didn't believe he could write a book. I remember exactly how much those doubts weighed on him before we began. He thought the process would take him years, that he'd get stuck halfway and never finish. **He thought the business would pull him in a thousand directions and he'd never be able to carve out the time.**

And, like so many entrepreneurs, he wondered whether anyone would really care about what he had to say.

The Turning Point

The turning point for Mark came when he realized that what he wished he'd had in his twenties—an experienced mentor to shorten the learning curve—was exactly what thousands of others needed today.

In the *Preface* of *Pocket Mentor*, he admitted:

> "I didn't have a mentor in my early twenties when I was starting Bull Outdoor Products. I learned every lesson the hard way. Although I could have used guidance from a seasoned pro, it wasn't available to me."

That absence became his motivation. He knew he couldn't go back and give his younger self the roadmap. But he could give it to others. Writing the book was no longer just about him—it was about service.

And once we reframed the project that way, the energy shifted.

The Process That Made the Book Possible

When Mark reflected on the journey, he realized the process of writing his book was far easier than he had ever imagined. With the structured support my team provided, he was able to get the thoughts out of his head and onto paper in a way that felt natural and productive. Each stage of progress gave him energy and momentum, turning what once felt overwhelming into something inspiring and enjoyable.

He discovered he didn't need to be a professional writer or wrestle with blank pages. All he had to do

was show up, share his stories, and trust the system we had in place. What once seemed like an impossible mountain became a clear, guided path forward.

Turning Business Challenges Into Lasting Influence

For Mark, the book became more than a collection of business advice—it was a bridge between his own entrepreneurial journey and the journeys of those just starting out. He retraced the path from his garage days, when he and his partner first spotted the spark of an idea for outdoor kitchens, through the scrappy hustle of leaving their spa manufacturing jobs, and into the early struggles of building Bull Outdoor Products. By sharing how the company grew from a small, uncertain venture into a recognized global brand, he invited readers to see not just the triumphs but also the bumps along the way.

What made the book powerful was that it wasn't written as a nostalgic memoir. Mark distilled decades of lessons into insights that mattered to his readers. He opened up about the mistakes he had made, showing how missteps could become stepping stones if handled with awareness and humility. He shared what it felt like to forge ahead without a mentor, and why he believed others shouldn't have to walk that lonely road without guidance. And he underscored the truth that success rarely arrives overnight—it comes through persistence, the willingness to stay focused, and the resilience to learn from criticism and setbacks.

By framing his personal experiences in this way, Mark transformed his own challenges into tools for others. The book didn't just tell his story; it allowed him to reframe the lessons of his past as a source of mentorship for future entrepreneurs. That honesty and openness became the reason *Pocket Mentor* resonated so deeply—it wasn't theory, it was lived experience, generously shared.

The Response That Erased His Doubts

When Mark first considered writing a book, his biggest doubts revolved around whether he had the ability to do it and whether anyone would truly value what he had to say. He had carried those questions for years, quietly wondering if the effort would be worth it. Yet when *Pocket Mentor* finally reached readers, their responses became the clearest evidence that his fears had been misplaced.

One reviewer admitted they wished the book had existed decades earlier, because it contained the kind of practical guidance that could have saved them from costly mistakes. Another, a seasoned entrepreneur, described feeling as though they were reliving their own journey through Mark's words, proof that his experiences spoke directly to the realities others faced. Readers pointed to the value of his honesty—his willingness to share not only strategies and successes but also failures—and recognized that this authenticity set the book apart.

The feedback showed Mark that he didn't need to have been a polished "writer" from the start. What mattered was that he had lived through challenges and was willing to lay them bare. Far from questioning his right to share his story, readers celebrated the fact that he had. In the end, the reviews became a mirror, reflecting back to Mark the very truth he had doubted: his voice was needed, and his story was a gift.

The Transformation: From Doubt to Impact

Looking back, what moves me most is how Mark went from almost giving up on the idea of writing, to holding his finished book in his hands, to seeing strangers online thanking him for helping them avoid mistakes.

He once thought he didn't have time to write. In the end, he realized he didn't have time **not** to write, because every year he delayed, there were entrepreneurs repeating errors he could have helped them avoid.

He once believed he wasn't a "writer." Now, his words are guiding thousands.

He once worried the book would drag on forever. Instead, the whole process was swift, focused, and—even in his words—fun.

The Regret He Doesn't Have to Live With

Perhaps the most powerful part of this story is what Mark doesn't have to carry: regret.

So many entrepreneurs dream of writing a book but never do. They wonder, "What if I had shared my story? What if my experiences could have helped someone else?" That haunting "what if" lingers.

Mark doesn't live with that weight. **He wrote *Pocket Mentor*. He launched it with a bang. He saw the impact on readers.** And he even got to experience the joy of gifting his book to people as a way of saying, "Here's what I've learned—use it to make your path easier."

Instead of regret, he gets to enjoy gratitude.

A Gift That Keeps on Giving

In the end, Mark was so thrilled with the results of his book that he sent me one of his top-tier Bull grills as a thank-you gift. Today, it sits proudly as the centerpiece of my garden. Whenever friends gather and compliment the barbecue, I always share Mark's story—how he once doubted he could ever write a book, how he overcame that belief, and how his words have gone on to inspire countless entrepreneurs. And of course, I never miss the chance to recommend *Pocket Mentor*, the book that made it all possible.

CHAPTER 13
Carl Grant III, CEO at Rainmakers Group

When I first met Carl Grant, I quickly understood why people listen when he speaks. His presence is calm yet compelling, with the confidence of someone who has spent decades at the top of professional services—and the humility of someone who knows there's always more to learn. He spoke with the candor of a man who has built, pioneered, and seen much, yet still feels called to put something greater into the world.

Carl wasn't looking to write a book just for the sake of being an author. For him, *How to Live the Abundant Life* was about answering an inner pull—something he describes as having "a book inside" that simply had to come out.

The Book Inside

Carl began writing essays years earlier, filling his computer with reflections and ideas. He published some on LinkedIn, but deep down he knew these scattered writings were only fragments. **He had more to say—about his faith, his relationships, his philosophy on abundance.**

But the task of writing a full book felt daunting. So he approached it piece by piece: first essays, then a podcast where he interviewed the best of the best in professional services. That podcast, which ran for fifty-three weeks, gave him both content and clarity. By the time it ended, Carl realized he was ready. The raw material for a book was there. What he needed was guidance to shape it.

For years, Carl had quietly researched who could help him publish. Leaders Brands kept bubbling to the surface. Still, committing was not easy. Like many people, he worried about paying for something and never seeing the promised result. But eventually, the weight of unrealized potential was heavier than the risk.

"It's like hiring a trainer at the gym," he told me. **"You know what you should do, but without someone guiding you, you won't do it."** So he made the leap—and found the process to be, in his words, everything it promised to be.

Doors the Book Opened

When the book finally launched, the ripple effects surprised even Carl. CEOs who normally would not have taken meetings invited him for coffee—because they had read his book. General counsels of Fortune 500 companies reached out. Consulting opportunities followed.

Then came an unexpected twist: while working in Saudi Arabia, Carl was asked to bring thirty copies of his book to a dinner with ministers from key government agencies. He watched as they accepted them—and later smiled when one of them left the very first review on Amazon's Saudi Arabia site.

The reach didn't stop there. A viral interview earned four million views, driving hundreds of book sales. Readers from

New Zealand wrote to him. Strangers posted his book on social media with heartfelt reviews. Some were moved enough to send him gifts—a new Fitbit, letters, tokens of gratitude. "I didn't expect that," Carl admitted. "But it showed me that the book was touching lives."

How the Book Impacted His Readers

If you look at the reviews on Amazon, you'll see that Carl's book struck a chord. Readers describe it as "inspiring," "practical," and "life-changing." One review notes how the book reminded them to "focus on people over possessions," a theme that threads through Carl's stories. Another highlights the simplicity of his advice—how he makes big concepts like abundance and fulfillment feel achievable in the everyday grind.

People aren't just reading the book; they're using it. One reviewer shared that they started applying Carl's tips on relationships and immediately noticed a difference in how they connected with their family and coworkers. Another mentioned that the book gave them a fresh sense of hope after a season of burnout.

That's the real measure of impact—not just the bestseller rankings Carl's book achieved, but readers who are actually living differently because of the words he put on the page.

The What-If He Never Faced

When I asked Carl to imagine the world where he never wrote his book, he paused. "I'd still be frustrated," he admitted. Frustrated that he had something inside him that never found its way out.

For him, the cost of not writing would have been far greater than the effort of writing. The book was his release, his contribution, his way of leaving something lasting behind.

Here's the most powerful part of Carl's story: because he wrote the book, he doesn't have to live with the regret of silence.

So many people carry around unspoken wisdom—lessons learned through pain, insights earned in the trenches—that never get shared. They go to the grave with their stories still inside them. Carl refused to let that happen.

By putting his life's lessons into *How to Live the Abundant Life*, he freed himself from the haunting thought: *What if I never shared this? What if the next generation has to learn it all the hard way?*

He doesn't have to wonder anymore. His message is out there. His words are in readers' hands. And every time someone leaves a review saying the book changed their perspective, Carl knows he made the right choice.

Carl Grant's journey reminds us that writing a book isn't about chasing prestige or padding a résumé. It's about solving problems that can't be solved any other way—capturing the lessons of a life so they can ripple outward to impact others.

He started with doubt, wrestled with vulnerability, and leaned on the support of family to push through. The result? A book that helps readers rethink abundance, live with more intention, and choose purpose over possessions.

Most importantly, Carl gets to live without regret. **He wrote the book. He shared his truth. And because of that, thousands of readers are now asking themselves how they, too, can live an abundant life.**

CHAPTER 14
Tamara Nall, CEO at The Leading Niche

When you first meet Tamara Nall, what strikes you is her warmth paired with a sharp, strategic mind. She isn't someone who simply runs a company—she *leads* with a vision that combines both rigor and humanity. As the CEO of The Leading Niche, a global management consulting firm, Tamara had already built a reputation for excellence. Yet, despite her success, there was a gap she couldn't close with boardroom strategies alone: how to package her thinking, experiences, and lessons in a way that could reach *thousands* of entrepreneurs and professionals beyond the immediate circle of her clients.

That's where her book came in.

Why a Book Was the Answer

Running a high-growth company, Tamara constantly met leaders who were brilliant at what they did but stuck in cycles of trial-and-error when it came to scaling, innovating, or even simply surviving in competitive markets. She saw the same issues repeating: great ideas stalling, teams losing focus, entrepreneurs missing out on growth because they didn't yet "think like" seasoned leaders.

Her challenge? She could solve these problems in one-on-one consulting engagements, but she couldn't be everywhere at once. She needed a platform that could extend her message beyond the walls of conference rooms and client calls. **A book wasn't just a nice idea—it was the only** medium that could crystallize her expertise into a lasting resource.

Making the Leap to Authorship

The decision didn't come lightly. Like many first-time authors, Tamara carried the quiet question: *Do I really have something to add to the crowded shelf of business books?* That's the limiting belief so many leaders face. She had seen colleagues dismiss the idea of writing because they felt underqualified or feared their story wouldn't resonate.

But Tamara leaned into a different truth: her story was *unique*. She wasn't recycling generic management tips—she was bringing to the table lessons forged in real boardroom battles, market challenges, and entrepreneurial leaps. She had led teams through multimillion-dollar growth and had the scars (and wisdom) to show for it.

Still, authorship demanded courage. Writing a book meant stepping out from behind the company brand and putting *herself* on the page. And that, in itself, is a leap most leaders hesitate to take.

The Breakthrough

With support from the publishing team, Tamara moved past hesitation. Her book, *Business Success Secrets: Entrepreneurial Thinking That Works*, was published—and quickly validated her leap. It went on to hit the ***Wall Street Journal* bestseller list**, won recognition at the **Miami Book Awards in 2022**, and earned **all five-star reviews on Amazon**.

What's striking is not just the awards, but what the book unlocked. Suddenly, she wasn't only a CEO—she was an *authoritative voice* in the broader business community. Opportunities opened that hadn't existed before: she got invited to prestigious events, her insights reached decision-makers she'd never met, and her reputation stretched far beyond consulting circles.

Impact on Readers

If you want to see the true impact of a book, you look at its readers. The Amazon reviews of *Business Success Secrets* tell a story all their own. Many describe it as "a must-read for entrepreneurs" and praise it for being "packed with practical advice." Again and again, readers emphasize how the book gave them clarity—whether in scaling their businesses, approaching leadership with greater confidence, or avoiding the common pitfalls that had previously held them back. One reviewer even shared that the book inspired them to "stop thinking small and start making bold moves," which is exactly the transformation Tamara hoped to spark.

Her book didn't just sit on shelves. It became a manual for action, a resource readers could turn to when they needed guidance or motivation. They walked away not only informed but energized and ready to apply what they had learned.

The Ripple Effects

The ripple effects of Tamara's authorship are remarkable. At the Miami Book Awards, she and her fellow authors were celebrated with the energy and prestige of the Grammys or the Olympics of publishing. Yet beyond the glamour of trophies and red carpets, the results were both practical and profound. Some of the co-authors who joined her on the project found that their consulting fees doubled almost overnight, while others were invited into new spheres of influence, including opportunities in academia—one was even considered for the position of dean at a university.

For Tamara herself, the book solidified her credibility in ways that went far beyond her consulting practice. It opened doors to ventures she had never envisioned and gave her clients and audiences a tangible resource they could rely on long after her keynote ended or a strategy session wrapped up.

The ripple extended even further when it came to her co-author Tomeka Holyfield. For Tomeka, the book was nothing short of transformational. She described it as the moment everything "leveled up." Becoming a *USA Today* and *Wall Street Journal* bestselling author instantly raised her visibility and shifted the trajectory of her career. Speaking fees that had once been modest tripled in value, new contracts and sponsorships poured in, and soon her standard keynote fee reached as high as $25,000. What had once seemed like an unattainable dream became her daily reality. Tomeka called the book "the project that keeps giving"—a defining pivot point that continues to shape her professional life.

That is the beauty of collaborative authorship: when one voice is amplified, the platform rises for everyone involved.

The Burden Lifted

Before writing the book, there was always the nagging thought: *What if my insights never reach the people who need them most?* For many leaders, that "what if" turns into regret later in life—the regret of knowledge that never got shared, of lessons that stayed locked in boardrooms instead of sparking transformation across industries.

Thanks to her book, Tamara will never live with that regret. She put her ideas into the world, and the world responded. Now, instead of wondering what might have been, she enjoys the satisfaction of seeing her work inspire entrepreneurs, guide business owners, and encourage new leaders to step boldly into their potential. And along the way, she also created a platform that lifted others, too.

CHAPTER 15
Andy Allen, Founder of The 80 Percent Project

When you meet Andy Allen, the first thing you'll notice is his energy. He's competitive, disciplined, and grounded in family and faith. But what makes Andy different is that **he's lived a life most people can only imagine—and then he decided to write a book about how he did it**, so others could do the same. His book, *The 80 Percent Project*, isn't just about achieving success. It's about redefining it. It's about living fully, intentionally, and without regrets.

The Challenge That Needed a Bigger Platform

Andy spent decades in real estate, rising to become one of the top agents in the country. Along the way, he saw something troubling: many of the most successful people he knew were also some of the unhappiest. They had sacrificed family, health, and personal joy on the altar of business. Andy knew from experience that this was unnecessary. His own life had been built around a very different model: prioritizing family first, carving out space for the things that truly matter, and letting work support that life, rather than consume it.

But here's the problem: Andy could only reach so many people through his coaching and personal network. The lessons he had learned from mentors like Gary Keller—lessons about intentional living, about building a "Life Pie" that balances family, work, finances, spirituality, and personal goals—were too valuable to stay confined to a small circle. He wanted to create change at scale, not just in individual conversations. And there was only one tool powerful enough to capture his philosophy, his stories, and his blueprint for transformation in a way that could reach people he would never meet in person: a book.

Why the Book Had to Be Written

For years, Andy carried the conviction that people needed a new model for success. He knew the myths all too well: that high-level success demands total sacrifice, that you can't have a thriving family and career, that "someday" you'll get around to living once you've earned enough. These were lies, and Andy had lived the proof. He wanted to show others how to claim what he called "the unimaginable life"—one where you succeed at work, but also in the areas that really matter.

Writing a book gave him the chance to codify what he'd been teaching his coaching clients for years: that success is intentional, that discipline is transferable, and that small, focused actions in the right areas can lead to generational change. His mission was bigger than sharing his story; it was about giving others permission to live differently.

Breaking Through His Own Barriers

You might think someone like Andy never struggled with doubts, but that wouldn't be true. At first, he questioned whether his story was really worth putting in a book. After all, he wasn't a billionaire or a household name. Would people care? Did he really have something new to add to the crowded field of success literature?

He also had to battle the subtle belief that writing a book wasn't "his thing." He was a real estate professional, a coach, a husband, a father—not an author. Like so many others, he had to shift from seeing himself as just a practitioner to recognizing that he had become a thought leader with a responsibility to share. As he admits in his acknowledgments, he needed nudging from people around him—mentors, marketing partners, and his family—to finally commit to the project.

Overcoming these limiting beliefs wasn't just about confidence. It was about purpose. Once Andy reframed the book as not being about him, but about the people he could help, the resistance dissolved. **Writing wasn't a vanity project; it was an act of service.**

The Doors the Book Opened

Publishing *The 80 Percent Project* changed the way Andy could show up in the world. It gave him a platform beyond coaching sessions and mastermind groups. It crystallized his ideas—the Life Pie, the 80/20 shift in priorities, the insistence on generational change—into a resource people could hold in their hands and return to again and again.

With the book, Andy could scale his influence. He could walk into a speaking engagement and know that his message wouldn't evaporate after the applause ended. Readers could take home his framework, implement it step by step, and share it with their families. **The book allowed him to**

multiply himself, to be in thousands of homes at once, quietly reshaping how people thought about success.

Readers' Transformations

The true measure of a book's value is in the lives it touches, and Andy's readers have been vocal about their transformations. Reviews of *The 80 Percent Project* describe it as a "blueprint to living an amazing life" and "a must-read for entrepreneurs." Readers highlight how it gave them clarity on balancing work and family, approaching leadership with confidence, and avoiding the trap of chasing success at the expense of life itself.

One reader shared that the book made them think differently about a few areas and reminded them that real happiness requires intentional focus on all areas of your life, not just financial goals. Others said it helped them finally see that discipline in one area of life (like fitness) could fuel breakthroughs in others. **For many, the book wasn't just informative—it was a wake-up call.** It gave them permission to prioritize joy, family, and purpose without guilt.

In short, Andy's book became more than just words on a page. It became a manual for action, a mirror reflecting what was possible, and a compass pointing toward a more intentional life.

No More What-Ifs

Before the book, Andy lived with a quiet frustration knowing that too many people were living lives of imbalance and regret, believing they had no choice—and that he had something to share but hadn't yet shared it at scale.

By writing *The 80 Percent Project*, Andy freed himself from that burden. **He no longer had to live with the regret of withholding his story.** He no longer had to wonder whether people could benefit from his experience. He had done his part: he had put the lessons into the world, where they could ripple outward for generations.

For Andy, this wasn't just about professional accomplishment. It was about peace of mind. He could look at his family, his clients, his readers, and know he had been intentional not just in how he lived, but in how he gave back. The book ensured that his philosophy wouldn't die with him; it would live on, shaping lives long after he was gone.

CHAPTER 16
Tom Fedro, Founder and CEO at Paragon Software Group

What Training Alone Couldn't Do

Tom Fedro had already achieved what most sales professionals only dream of. He had years of experience closing multi-million-dollar deals in high-tech software. His desk was full of notes, folders, and outlines of stories he wanted to share. He had the training, the wins, and the credibility. What he didn't have was a book.

Like many professionals, Tom fell into the trap of "someday." He told himself again and again that he would write a book when things slowed down, when the timing was right, when he finally got around to it. But the years passed, and nothing changed. He still had the same notes, the same folders, the same idea.

Training had given him skills, but training alone couldn't create a finished book.

What Made the Difference

The shift came from an unexpected place: his father. At ninety-three, his dad was a World War II and Korean War veteran who didn't really understand what Tom did for a living. Tom's work in global software sales—negotiating deals with Germans, Chinese, and others who had once been wartime adversaries—made no sense to him.

Tom wanted to give his father something tangible, something that explained his life's work in a way his dad could hold and be proud of. That urgency made him realize the truth: nothing would change until he committed.

"I knew I was going to have to write a check," Tom said. Once he did, everything shifted. Partnering with Leaders Brands gave him the structure, accountability, and professional team he needed to turn years of intention into a finished book.

The Mindset Shift

Writing the check wasn't just a financial transaction. It was a mindset shift. Until that point, the book had been optional. Afterward, it became inevitable.

"Once I wrote the check, everything came together," Tom explained. It forced him to treat the project as real, not as a vague "someday" dream. Suddenly, scheduling calls, reviewing drafts, and pushing through revisions weren't chores—they were commitments he had paid for, milestones he was determined to complete.

Without that forcing function, he admitted he would still be stuck. "I would have been one of those guys telling people for another ten years, 'I'm going to write a book someday.'" The difference between talking and doing was the check.

What Became Possible

From there, possibilities opened up that Tom couldn't have anticipated. Holding the book in his hands was surreal. Seeing it on Amazon, climbing the bestseller lists, and racking up reviews was thrilling. Suddenly, his years of experience weren't just in his head or on scraps of paper—they were in a published, respected book that anyone could access.

The impact went beyond the emotional. The book transformed his professional credibility. Prospects and peers would look him up on Amazon mid-conversation and say, "Holy smoke, this is real." **He wasn't just another sales guy with stories—he was an authority who had codified his process in print.**

The book also led to new introductions, masterminds, and partnerships. Tom found himself in rooms and conversations he would not have been invited to otherwise. The book became his calling card, his proof of expertise, his entry point into opportunities.

What It Meant to Readers

Readers didn't just buy the book—they used it. The reviews that came in were overwhelmingly positive, filled with stories of sales professionals who applied his repeatable process to win larger, more complex deals.

The book wasn't just another title on a crowded shelf. It was practical, valuable, and actionable. For many readers, it was the bridge between struggling with unpredictable results and mastering a method that delivered consistency. Each review was validation: Tom's work was helping people he had never even met.

The Ripple Effect

The ripple effect extended far beyond business. Tom gave the very first copy to his father on Father's Day. His dad proudly carried it around his assisted living community, showing it to everyone he met. Just four months later, his father passed away. Tom was deeply grateful he had finished the book in time. **"Thank you, Lord, that I got this done,"** he said.

The book also touched his family in another way. Both of his sons followed him into sales, and his oldest recently closed a $7.7 million software deal. Tom sees the book as part of the legacy he is passing on—not just to readers, but to his own children.

Even six years after publication, the book continues to build credibility, spark conversations, and influence his network. It sits on his shelf as a reminder that he didn't just dream about writing a book—he made the decision, wrote the check, and got it done.

The lesson is clear: without writing the check, Tom would still be stuck in "someday." With it, he became an author, an authority, and a man who turned intention into impact.

Write the check. Get it done. Don't just dream—decide.

CHAPTER 17
Alinka Rutkowska, Co-Founder of Leaders Brands

Before the Book

When I sat down to write my first book, back in 2010, I wasn't the founder of Leaders Brands. I wasn't a publishing strategist, and I certainly wasn't someone with hundreds of thousands of book sales behind me. I was simply someone with an idea that wouldn't let me go—and a head full of doubts.

Maybe you've felt them too.

I don't have the time to write.
Who am I to write a book? I'm not a famous name.
What if nobody reads it?
What if it's not good enough?

These weren't abstract worries. They felt real, heavy, and paralyzing. Each time I thought about writing, another excuse popped into my mind. At one point, I convinced myself I should wait until I was more "ready," whatever that meant.

The truth was, I was scared. Scared of wasting time. Scared of failing. Scared of being judged.

And here's the irony: those are the same fears I now hear every day from leaders who come to me for help. They sound reasonable—*too busy, too risky, too uncertain*—but at their core, they're all the same thing: fear dressed up as logic.

If I had listened to those fears, I wouldn't be writing this book. And none of the other chapters you've just read—Tom Fedro, Po Chung, Tamara Nall, or any of the others—would have happened either.

Because the only reason I was able to attract these extraordinary leaders into my orbit is that I wrote that first book.

But I didn't know that at the time. All I knew was that the excuses were loud, and the only way forward was to write anyway.

The Turning Point

The shift didn't happen in some dramatic movie moment where the skies opened and everything suddenly made sense. It happened in a simple conversation with a mentor—one I almost brushed off at the time.

I was voicing all my doubts again. "I don't know if I'm ready. Maybe I should wait. What if it flops?" I rattled off excuse after excuse, each one sounding perfectly logical in my head.

My mentor just listened. Patiently. And then he leaned forward and said six words that stopped me in my tracks:

"Winners find ways. Losers find excuses."

That was it. No long lecture. No motivational speech. Just one sentence that hit me like a punch in the gut.

I went quiet. Because deep down, I knew he was right. I had been dressing up my fear as strategy, decorating my hesitation with logic. But at the end of the day, they were excuses.

And excuses don't write books. Excuses don't change lives. Excuses don't leave legacies.

I remember sitting with that sentence for days. It followed me around like an echo: *Winners find ways. Losers find excuses.* Was I really going to let myself be on the wrong side of that divide?

That was the moment I stopped negotiating with my excuses. I decided that if I wanted to be in the winner's circle—the one percent who actually publish—then I had to find a way. Any way. Even if it was messy. Even if it was imperfect. Even if it scared me.

And so I did. Page by page, draft by draft, I found ways. Sometimes clumsy ones. Sometimes painful ones. But they added up. And eventually, they added up to a book.

Today, when I work with leaders who are struggling with the same limiting beliefs I once carried, I often hear that same tone in their voice. The hesitation. The rational-sounding excuses. The fear hiding under the surface. And when I hear it, I share what my mentor once told me:

"Winners find ways. Losers find excuses."

It's blunt. Some flinch when they hear it. But most know, deep down, it's the truth they've been avoiding. And for many of them, just like it was for me, that one line becomes the turning point.

Because at the end of the day, writing a book isn't about perfect timing, unlimited resources, or fear magically disappearing. It's about making a choice: will you find a way, or will you keep finding excuses?

That choice is the only real turning point. Everything else flows from it.

The Book That Built My Future

When I finally got past my excuses and wrote my book, I thought the biggest outcome would be sales. And yes, the sales came—tens of thousands of copies, to the point where I eventually wrote *How I Sold 80,000 Books*, which today has more than a thousand reviews. But sales weren't the true result.

The real result was everything that the book set in motion. It gave me credibility I could never have manufactured any other way. It gave me a voice in rooms I wouldn't have been invited into. It put me on podcasts, on other people's summits, and in the pages of publications like *Forbes* and *Entrepreneur*. Suddenly, I wasn't the one chasing opportunities—opportunities were finding me.

That first book became the foundation for the work I do today—helping leaders like you transform their ideas into books that change the trajectory of their lives.

Since then, I've helped more than 500 clients step into authorship. Together, we've launched hundreds of books that went on to become *USA Today*, *Wall Street Journal*, and USA National Bestsellers. I've guided authors whose books went on to win awards, whose businesses expanded far beyond what they had before, whose speaking fees climbed as high as $25,000 per keynote, and whose projects attracted the investors they needed to move forward. By showing leaders how to capture their ideas, publish strategically, and launch with impact, I've seen again and again how a book can transform not only authority, but also the opportunities and growth that follow.

What makes me proud isn't just those achievements themselves, but what they represent. Every one of those wins started in the same place I once found myself—staring at a blank page, full of reasons not to begin. And every one of those leaders made the same choice I made: to stop buying into excuses and start building their legacy.

That's what books do. They don't just sit on shelves. **They open doors, start conversations, attract opportunities,** and change the people who write them as much as the people who read them.

For me, they've created not only a business that lets me work with extraordinary leaders, but also a life I once thought was out of reach. My books have allowed me to provide for my family, to run a company that matters, and to live my dream life—all because I decided to act instead of hiding behind excuses.

And that's why I know the same is possible for you. Because I've lived it, I've seen it, and I've helped hundreds of others do the same.

The Truth That Changed Everything

Looking back now, I can see something I couldn't when I was sitting there with a blank page and a head full of doubts. The excuses were never really about time or money or readiness. They were about fear. Fear of failing. Fear of looking foolish. Fear of putting myself out there and not being enough.

Your Book or Your Excuse

When my mentor said, **"Winners find ways. Losers find excuses."** I didn't like hearing it at the time—it was blunt, even a little harsh. But it was true. And once I let those words sink in, I realized I had a choice: either keep telling myself stories about why I couldn't do it, or finally write the book that would change my life.

I chose to write. And everything that followed—the sales, the media features, the stage invitations, the incredible leaders I now get to work with every day—happened because I made that one decision.

That's why, when I talk to future clients and hear the same hesitation in their voices, I share that line with them. Not to be critical, but to offer them the same wake-up call I once needed. Because every excuse, no matter how polished it sounds, comes down to the same question: **Are you going to find a way, or are you going to settle for an excuse?**

I know which side I chose. And I know which side I want you to choose. Because if you let excuses win, nothing changes. But if you find a way—even if it's messy, even if it's imperfect, even if it's scary—that book might just open doors you can't even see yet.

That's the lesson I learned—and the one I pass on now: **Winners find ways. Losers find excuses.**

PART III

Winners Find Ways, Losers Find Excuses

Why 99 Percent Will Never Have a Book

The truth is, **most people will never publish a book.** Not because they couldn't—but because they don't think like leaders. They tell themselves they'll do it "someday." They settle for being doers, not thought leaders. They let limiting beliefs dictate their future instead of claiming authority now.

Only the one percent ever make it to authorship—and that one percent dominates conversations, shapes industries, and leaves legacies—while the rest are forgotten or defined by others.

Before every remarkable author you've just read about could enjoy the doors their book opened, they had to confront the same doubts you might be wrestling with right now.

They had to silence the voice whispering, *"Not now. Not me. Not yet."*

Authority always comes with resistance. The difference is that **leaders push through, while the 99 percent retreat.**

Let's look at the most common excuses—and why none of them should stop you. **Because when you're in the one percent, you find ways. And deep down, you already know right now whether you are… or you're not.**

CHAPTER 18
"I Don't Have Time"

You might be thinking: "All these leaders you write about—they must've had spare hours in their days." The reality is, they were just as busy as you are. The difference? **They decided the book was a priority—not an optional side project.**

How many people do you think come to me and say they want to write a book because they're bored? Exactly—nobody. Nobody ever sits down to write a book because they have nothing else going on. The people who come to me are CEOs, executives, entrepreneurs, founders, and investors. They are already running businesses, leading teams, juggling deals, managing families, speaking at events, and flying around the world. They have every reason in the world to say, *"I don't have time."*

But here's what separates them from the 99 percent: they choose to create time. They see the book not as a side hustle, but as an extension of their leadership. They know it's an asset that will work for them 24/7—winning clients, commanding stages, attracting media—even when they're busy doing something else.

So no, leaders don't write books because they're bored. They write books because they can't afford *not* to. They make time because they understand that a book isn't another project on the list—it's the project that elevates everything else.

Let's look at a few examples to see how it's done in practice.

Leo Tolstoy: Making Writing a Habit

Have you heard of Leo Tolstoy? He's often remembered as one of the greatest novelists in history, the author of *War and Peace* and *Anna Karenina*. But what's less talked about is how he managed to produce such monumental works while living a life packed with responsibility. Tolstoy wasn't a quiet recluse with endless free time. He was a husband, the father of 13 children, the manager of a large estate, a reformer in education, and an outspoken public thinker.

So how did he do it? He **got his priorities straight.**

Tolstoy kept meticulous journals where he recorded not only his daily activities but also his "rules of life." He woke early, blocked time to read and write, and treated the act of putting words on paper as non-negotiable. He once noted that he had to write every single day "without fail, not so much for the success of the work, as in order not to get out of my routine." That discipline is what allowed him to produce works that still influence literature, politics, and philosophy centuries later.

And here's the striking truth: Tolstoy isn't remembered for how well he managed his estate or for the educational reforms he championed. He's remembered for his thought leadership preserved in writing. His books are what carried his voice far beyond his lifetime.

The Prime Minister Who Made Time to Write

If anyone ever had the right to say, "I don't have time to write," it was Winston Churchill. When most people think of Winston Churchill, they picture the wartime Prime Minister of Britain, the bulldog spirit, the "We shall fight on the beaches" speech. He led a nation through one of history's darkest hours, shouldering a burden that would crush most men. He was making life-and-death decisions daily, meeting with generals and world leaders, managing a government in crisis. If anyone had an excuse to say, *"I don't have time to write,"* it was Churchill.

And yet, Churchill wrote. Constantly. Over his lifetime, he produced more than **forty books, thousands of articles, and millions of words.** He turned his reflections, strategies, and observations into multi-volume histories, biographies, and memoirs. Writing wasn't a hobby squeezed into spare hours—it was a discipline he made time for, even while holding one of the most demanding jobs on earth.

Here's the part that most people miss: **Churchill's single greatest international recognition didn't come from politics or even from leading Britain to victory in World War II.** His highest honor was the **Nobel Prize in Literature, awarded in 1953.** Think about that. A man who was Prime Minister during the Blitz, who rallied the free world against fascism, is remembered in history books with a gold medallion not for his governance, but for his writing.

The Nobel committee praised him "for his mastery of historical and biographical description as well as for brilliant oratory in defending exalted human values." In other words, it wasn't just what Churchill did that mattered. It was that he **captured it in words that would endure.** Generals won battles. Politicians passed laws. But Churchill wrote the record. That's why his voice still echoes, decades later, not just in history classrooms but in leadership seminars, boardrooms, and strategy discussions.

And here's the kicker: Churchill's legacy is portable because of his books. Without them, he would be remembered as a wartime prime minister, yes, but probably one of many. With them, he is remembered as one of history's greatest communicators and thinkers—a man whose ideas live beyond his life.

So ask yourself: if Churchill, running a nation at war, found the time to write, what's your excuse? He didn't wait for "someday." He didn't say, "I'll get to it when things calm down." He wrote while the bombs were falling, while the war was raging, while history was unfolding. Because he knew that without writing, the story could slip away, or worse, be told by someone else.

That Nobel Prize is the ultimate proof. Churchill's greatest global recognition wasn't about the office he held or the battles he oversaw. It was about the words he left behind. Words that still lead, long after the man is gone.

Phil Knight: Building Nike *and* Writing *Shoe Dog*

Phil Knight had every reason to say he didn't have time to write. By the time most people first heard his name, Nike was already a global empire. But Knight's story began long before the swoosh became an icon. He was a scrappy entrepreneur, fresh out of business school, running around Japan to secure shoe distribution rights, selling sneakers from the trunk of his car, and negotiating manufacturing deals that could make or break his fledgling company.

As Nike grew, so did his responsibilities. Knight wasn't just running a small team—he was steering one of the fastest-growing companies in the world. He was competing against established giants like Adidas and Reebok, navigating global supply chains, managing investors, handling lawsuits, and fighting PR battles. Every decision felt high stakes. Every day was full.

If anyone had an airtight excuse to say, "I don't have time to write a book," it was Phil Knight.

And yet, he wrote one.

Knight didn't write *Shoe Dog* because he was bored or finally had nothing else on his plate. He wrote it because he understood something critical: **if he didn't tell the story of Nike, someone else would.**

By the time he sat down to work on *Shoe Dog,* journalists had written countless articles about Nike's successes and controversies. Biographers had speculated about him. Critics had weighed in. But none of them could capture the truth the way he could. And that's the same crossroads every leader faces: either you control the narrative, or someone else writes it for you.

Knight chose to take control. He didn't delegate the story of Nike to historians or competitors. He made time to write it himself.

Your Book or Your Excuse

When *Shoe Dog* was published in 2016, it wasn't just another business memoir. It was raw, vulnerable, and honest in ways most corporate books aren't. Knight didn't sugarcoat the challenges. He wrote about near-bankruptcy, fierce competitors, personal doubts, and the mistakes that could have sunk the company.

The book struck a nerve. It became an instant **New York Times bestseller,** selling millions of copies worldwide. Bill Gates called it one of the best books he had ever read, and it quickly earned a place on business school syllabi, executive reading lists, and in startup incubators.

Why? Because *Shoe Dog* wasn't just about shoes. It was about the grit, resilience, and vision required to build something lasting. It was about leadership under pressure. It was about making time for what matters most, even when you feel like you don't have a second to spare.

And here's the kicker: Knight will be remembered not for the endless meetings he led, the logistics problems he solved, or the contracts he signed. He'll be remembered for **the story he captured in writing.** Nike might have been his business legacy, but *Shoe Dog* became his thought leadership legacy.

Maybe you're tempted to say, *"That's different. Knight had resources. He had a team."* True—but resources don't create time. If anything, running a billion-dollar brand only made him busier. The only way *Shoe Dog* got written is because Knight **made it a priority.**

And that's the difference between the 99 percent and the one percent. The 99 percent wait for free time that never comes.

The one percent carve it out. They know that one book will do more for their legacy than a thousand emails or meetings.

Knight could have skipped writing his book and left the world to interpret Nike's story without him. But by making time, he took control of the narrative—and turned it into one of the most respected business books ever written.

So ask yourself: if Phil Knight could run Nike and still write, what's your excuse?

CHAPTER 19
"It's Too Expensive"

When people say, "I don't have the money," what they're really saying is, "I'm not willing to be resourceful." As Tony Robbins puts it, the defining factor isn't resources—it's **resourcefulness.** In a previous chapter, I shared that a mentor once told me, **"Winners find ways. Losers find excuses."**

Resourcefulness over Resources: The Jobs Lesson

Would we have the iPhone if Steve Jobs hadn't gotten resourceful? Think about that for a moment.

Jobs didn't grow up with wealth or security. He was adopted as a baby, raised by a machinist father and a bookkeeper mother in a modest California household. His upbringing wasn't about privilege—it was about making do, tinkering, and dreaming. As a teenager, he spent hours hanging around the Homebrew Computer Club and local garages, fascinated by electronics and hungry to create something bigger than himself. There was no trust fund waiting for him. No wealthy backer ready to underwrite his ideas.

When he and his friend Steve Wozniak decided to build their first computer, they had the vision but not the resources. They could have said, *"We'll wait until the money comes. We'll wait until we're ready.*"That's what most people would do. But they weren't most people.

Jobs sold his Volkswagen van. Wozniak sold his prized Hewlett-Packard calculator. These weren't casual decisions. That van was Jobs' freedom. That calculator was Wozniak's most valued tool. They gave them up because they believed the outcome was worth more than what they owned at the moment. Those two sacrifices gave them just enough to buy the parts to build what became the **Apple I.**

It wasn't glamorous. It wasn't safe. But it was a start. And that start changed everything. Here's the truth: if they had thrown their hands in the air and said, "We don't have money, so we can't do this," the world would look very different today. There would be no Apple II to kickstart the personal computer revolution. No Macintosh to redefine design and user experience. No iPod to change how we consume music. No iPhone to reshape culture, communication, and business itself.

Think about that: the device in your pocket, the apps you use every day, the way you connect with the world—none of it would exist if two young men hadn't decided to get resourceful.

Jobs and Wozniak didn't let their lack of privilege or money define their future. They didn't treat cost as a barrier. They treated it as a challenge to solve. That's the mark of leadership. That's resourcefulness in action.

Now put yourself in their shoes. You have a vision—a book that could elevate your authority, open doors, win clients, leave a legacy. You could look at the price tag and say, "It's too expensive. Maybe later." Or you could get resourceful, find a way, and set in motion something that shapes not just your business, but your identity as a leader.

Because leaders don't wait for perfect conditions. They create them. And the world remembers them for it.

Howard Schultz: Refusing to Take "No" for an Answer

When Howard Schultz first imagined Starbucks, it wasn't anything like the chain you know today. Back then, in the early 1980s, Starbucks was just a small Seattle company selling roasted beans and equipment. Schultz, then the company's marketing director, traveled to Milan, Italy, and had an experience that changed his life. He stood at the espresso bars in Milan, watching people linger over coffee, talking, connecting, doing business, building community. It wasn't about grabbing a quick cup. It was about the *experience*.

Schultz came back to the US convinced that Starbucks could be more than just beans. It could be a *third place*—not home, not work, but the gathering spot in between. A place where coffee wasn't just a product, but a ritual.

But there was a problem. Investors didn't see it. He pitched his vision over and over, and what he heard back was rejection. "Americans won't pay $2 for coffee." "Nobody wants Italian-style espresso culture here." "It's too risky."

Dozens of investors said no.

Most people would have given up. Most people would have thought, *Maybe they're right. Maybe it's not realistic.* But Schultz refused to fold. He knew what he had seen in Milan. He knew how it made him feel. He knew people would pay not just for coffee, but for the experience.

Here's where Schultz showed the difference between the 99 percent and the one percent. Instead of letting those rejections define him, he got resourceful. He started cobbling together money from people he knew. He pitched friends. He pitched family. He asked again and again.

It wasn't glamorous. And it wasn't easy. Imagine being in his shoes: every "no" cutting at your confidence, each rejection suggesting maybe you were crazy. But Schultz leaned into persistence. He treated every no as fuel. Every door closed only made him knock harder on the next one.

Eventually, through sheer grit, he raised the $1.25 million he needed to buy Starbucks from its founders and reimagine it around his vision. That was the tipping point.

Think about it. Every time you see someone holding a Starbucks cup in an airport, on a city street, or in a boardroom, you're witnessing the legacy of someone who refused to let "too expensive" be the final word. Schultz could have said, *"I can't raise the money. I'll wait."* But he didn't. He kept asking. He kept moving. He made it happen.

Schultz didn't have unlimited resources. He didn't have guaranteed backing. He didn't have certainty. But he had resourcefulness. And that's what leaders have in common: they find ways when others stop.

So when you say, "Publishing a book is too expensive," what you're really saying is, "I'm not willing to get resourceful."

Howard Schultz built Starbucks by refusing to give up on his vision and refusing to let money—or the lack of it—stand in his way. You may not be building a coffee empire. But you are building authority, visibility, and legacy. And just like Schultz, the difference between having it and not having it comes down to resourcefulness.

Because winners don't let "too expensive" be the excuse. Winners, like Schultz, find ways.

Walt Disney: No Money, No Backing, No Excuses

When you think of Walt Disney today, you probably think of an empire—Disney World, blockbuster films, global merchandising, and a brand that defines childhood itself. But that's the end of the story, not the beginning. The beginning looked very different.

Walt Disney grew up in a poor family in Missouri. His father struggled to hold down work, and Walt picked up odd jobs as a teenager just to get by. He had no financial cushion, no family wealth, and no powerful connections waiting to open doors. What he did have was a pencil, imagination, and the stubborn belief that he could make a living by drawing.

After working briefly in advertising, Walt started his first animation studio in Kansas City—Laugh-O-Gram Films. He scraped by producing short reels for local businesses, but the company never gained solid footing. By 1923, it collapsed into bankruptcy. He was broke, embarrassed, and barely able to pay rent. Most people in his position would have given up.

Your Book or Your Excuse

But Walt didn't quit. He packed a cardboard suitcase, borrowed **$40 from a friend**, and took a train to Los Angeles. No investors. No stable job. No backup plan. Just the conviction that he could start over.

In Los Angeles, Walt teamed up with his brother Roy. They set up shop in their uncle's garage, cobbling together a "studio" with a borrowed camera and secondhand furniture. Their first projects weren't glamorous—low-budget shorts and advertising reels. But they treated them as stepping stones.

What they lacked in resources, they replaced with hustle. Walt pitched relentlessly. He leaned on personal contacts. He reinvested every dollar back into the business. And slowly, small opportunities began to come their way.

Their first real breakthrough was a short series featuring a live-action girl interacting with cartoons—the *Alice Comedies*. That got the attention of distributors and gave them a small but critical income stream. It wasn't riches, but it was momentum.

Then came another setback. Walt created a new character, Oswald the Lucky Rabbit, under contract with Universal. But in a ruthless move, Universal seized control of the character and poached most of Walt's animators. Overnight, Walt lost his star character and much of his team.

Most people would have folded at that point. Bankruptcy once. Betrayal twice. No capital. No security. Every logical reason to quit.

But on the train ride back from New York, Disney sketched a new character in his notebook: a cheerful little mouse. That mouse, first called Mortimer and later renamed Mickey, became the foundation of the Disney empire.

Disney took another risk: he poured everything into making *Steamboat Willie* in 1928, one of the first cartoons with synchronized sound. At the time, sound in film was brand new and expensive. Walt had no money to spare, but he found a way—leveraging loans, begging favors, and stretching every resource.

When *Steamboat Willie* premiered, it was an instant sensation. The audience loved Mickey Mouse. Disney suddenly had not just a cartoon, but a character, a brand, and a future. From there came innovations like *Snow White and the Seven Dwarfs*—the first full-length animated feature, which critics predicted would bankrupt him again. Instead, it became a massive hit.

What makes Disney's story matter to you isn't just that he succeeded. It's how he succeeded. **He had every excuse not to.** No money. No investors. Bankruptcy. Losing his intellectual property. If anyone had reason to say, "It's too expensive, I'll wait until I have the resources," it was Walt Disney.

But he didn't wait. He found ways. He borrowed. He improvised. He bet on himself, again and again. And because of that, Disney became more than a man. He became a symbol of imagination and leadership that lives on long after him.

So here's the question: are you telling yourself it's too expensive to publish a book, that you don't have the resources right now?

Your Book or Your Excuse

Remember Disney. He started with a borrowed $40, a garage, and a drawing of a mouse. The Disney empire was built not because he had resources, but because he refused to let their absence be the excuse.

When you tell yourself you'll wait until you have more money, more certainty, or more backing, you're thinking like the 99 percent who never move. The one percent—the Disneys of the world—act with what they have, and build the rest along the way.

Because winners don't wait for resources. Winners get resourceful.

CHAPTER 20
"I Need to Talk To..."

One of the most common delays leaders bring up when faced with the opportunity to write their book is: "I need to talk to my partner." At first glance, it sounds respectful. After all, you share a life, maybe a home, maybe finances. But peel back the layer, and often it's not about respect at all. It's about hesitation. It's about fear wearing the mask of partnership.

Of course, some decisions should involve your partner—especially those that affect shared commitments. But there's a difference between *consulting* and *deferring*. One strengthens trust; the other quietly erodes your confidence.

Because let's be honest: the book is your voice, your authority, your legacy. Passing the decision to someone else might feel safer in the moment, but what does it really mean long term?

Whose Responsibility Is It?

Imagine the decision as a coin in your hand. One side says yes, the other says no. You're ready to flip it, but the coin feels heavier than usual. This isn't dinner plans or a vacation—this is your career, your visibility, your future. The weight makes you hesitate, so you slide the coin across the table to your partner.

But ask yourself: who reaps the benefits if the book succeeds—you or them? Who bears the consequences if it doesn't—you or them? Whose name is on the cover? Whose authority is cemented? Right—it's you.

So why give away the coin? Isn't it your responsibility to make the call when you're the one living with the outcome? Isn't that what leadership is: the willingness to own decisions because you're the one accountable for their results?

Now face the real test. **What happens if your partner says no?** Do you go ahead anyway? If so, then you didn't need their permission—you needed your own courage. Or do you shrink back and drop the project? If that's the case, then admit what's happening: you're giving away your voice to avoid the discomfort of deciding.

And what will that cost you? Lost opportunities. Delayed authority. A future shaped not by conviction but by hesitation. Responsibility doesn't vanish just because you hand it away—it always circles back. The only question is whether you'll carry it now with strength, or later with regret.

Why Do You Need to Run It by Someone Else?

Think about the decisions you already make. You sign contracts. You approve budgets. You hire staff. You take risks daily. You don't stop to ask permission for each move—you're trusted to lead.

So why now, when it comes to writing your book, do you suddenly need to check in?

Is it that your partner doesn't trust you? If that's true, is that really the kind of partnership you want—where you're trusted with your business but not with your own story? Or is it you who doesn't fully trust yourself, and you're hoping their "no" will save you from having to risk a "yes"?

Ask yourself directly: if they say no, what happens? Do you still move forward, because deep down you know this matters? Then why ask in the first place? Or do you back down, swallow your voice, and convince yourself the timing isn't right? In that case, what are you really choosing—avoiding failure, or guaranteeing regret?

Notice the pattern. When you pass the decision off, you're not protecting the relationship. You're protecting yourself. You're creating an escape hatch in case things don't work out. But isn't that the opposite of what you demand of your team? Don't you expect them to act with conviction, to make decisions, to take responsibility?

So which story do you want to live—the leader who asks for permission, or the leader who seeks input, then decides? One story ends with progress, the other with silence. Which feels more like you?

Do You Want to Resent Your Partner?

Now picture this. A year passes. A colleague in your industry launches their book. They're invited on stage at the conference you've been eyeing. They're interviewed on the podcast you listen to. They're everywhere. And you sit in the audience thinking, *That could have been me.*

Your Book or Your Excuse

Whose fault will you say it was? Theirs, for not supporting you? Or yours, for handing them a decision that was always yours to make?

Because here's the truth. If they say no and you do it anyway, you prove what was real all along: this was your decision. If they say no and you don't do it, then every door that stays closed will feel like their fault—but really, it's yours. That bitterness doesn't disappear; it grows. First, it's quiet: *If only they had supported me.* Then it festers: *They held me back.* Eventually, you realize you're not resenting them—you're resenting yourself.

Isn't it more respectful to say, "I've decided to do this, and here's how I'll protect our life together," than to show up uncertain and later accuse them of being the reason you never followed through? Isn't it better to invite them into your celebration than cast them as the villain in your silence?

So ask yourself: when they say no, will you do it anyway? If yes, then start now. Stop pretending you need permission. If no, then be honest—you're not choosing harmony. You're choosing resentment. And you're choosing it knowingly.

Which future do you want—the one where you launch and celebrate together, or the one where you sit quietly, nursing the regret of never taking your shot?

Because in the end, that decision is still your coin. You can flip it now—or let it sit in someone else's hand forever.

CHAPTER 21
"I'll Publish After…"

This objection comes in many disguises. Maybe you've said it to yourself one of these ways:

- ❏ "My story isn't big enough."
- ❏ "I haven't achieved enough yet."
- ❏ "I don't have anything new to say."
- ❏ "Why would anyone care about my story?"
- ❏ "I'm not famous enough."
- ❏ "I need more success first."
- ❏ "My journey is still ongoing."
- ❏ "I don't want to sound like I'm bragging."

Different words, same hesitation: **you don't feel worthy of publishing.** You think authority is reserved for people who already have a Fortune 500 logo on their résumé, a TV show, or a billionaire net worth. But the truth is, that's not what readers want. **Readers don't need you to be "done." They need you to be useful.**

Tim Ferriss: From 26 Rejections to Global Authority

When you look at Tim Ferriss today, it's easy to think he was destined for success. He's a household name in entrepreneurship and self-improvement, the author of multiple bestselling books, and the host of one of the most downloaded podcasts in the world. But rewind to 2006, and the picture was very different. Ferriss wasn't famous. He wasn't a CEO of a major company. He didn't have a massive platform or millions of fans waiting to buy his book. He was simply a guy with some unconventional ideas about work, time, and lifestyle.

At the time, Ferriss was running a nutritional supplements business, and he had noticed a frustrating pattern in his life and in the lives of people around him: they were working harder and harder, chasing some imagined "later" when life would finally get good. Retirement, travel, freedom—all of it was pushed into the future, sacrificed for the grind of the present. Ferriss thought there was another way, and he wanted to share it. He started writing the manuscript that would eventually become *The 4-Hour Workweek*.

If you've ever worried your story isn't big enough, here's the moment you'll relate to most: when Ferriss started pitching his book, publishers didn't see a breakout hit. They didn't see a rising thought leader. They saw risk. One by one, they rejected him. Not just a few. Twenty-six publishers said no. That's twenty-six industry professionals telling him his idea wasn't good enough, his story wasn't compelling enough, his book wouldn't sell.

Most people would have quit right there. They would have taken the rejection as proof that they were right all along: *my story isn't big enough, I'm not qualified, I should wait until I've achieved more.* But Ferriss didn't quit. He pushed forward because he understood something essential: **a story doesn't need to be "big" to matter. It needs to be relevant.**

Ferriss didn't have a glamorous résumé. He had lived experiments—testing productivity hacks, rethinking work, exploring travel, and building a small business differently. Those experiences weren't headline-worthy, but they were *useful*. They spoke directly to the frustrations millions of people were feeling but hadn't put into words.

When *The 4-Hour Workweek* finally launched in 2007, readers didn't flock to it because Ferriss was famous. They flocked to it because he gave them a new way of seeing their own lives. He showed them it was possible to design life differently. The authority didn't come from his status—it came from the usefulness of his perspective.

That's the point too many leaders miss. You think you need a billion-dollar exit, a global empire, or a title on the cover of *Forbes* to make your story worth telling. But readers aren't looking for a résumé. They're looking for a lens. They want to see themselves in your story, and they want you to help them reframe what's possible.

Ferriss' story proves that what you think of as "not big enough" may be exactly what makes your book powerful. Ordinary struggles, real experiments, and the courage to challenge norms connect more deeply than polished success stories ever do.

So ask yourself: are you holding back because you think your story isn't big enough—or are you ready to realize that size doesn't matter, resonance does?

Because if Ferriss had waited until he was "big enough," we would have no *4-Hour Workweek*, no movement, no millions of lives changed.

Authority didn't follow size. Size followed publishing.

Reid Hoffman: Don't Wait Until "After"

One of the most common excuses leaders tell themselves is, "I'll publish after I sell my company. After the big exit. After I've achieved enough to really have a story." On the surface, it sounds reasonable. Why not wait until the résumé looks perfect? But the truth is, waiting costs you years of influence, visibility, and opportunity. And no one proves that better than Reid Hoffman.

Reid Hoffman is best known as the co-founder of LinkedIn, the professional networking platform that transformed how the business world connects. But when he published his first major book, *The Startup of You* in 2012, LinkedIn was still growing. It wasn't yet the household name it would become. The company had gone public the year before, but Hoffman was still deeply involved in building, scaling, and shaping its future. He didn't wait until after. He wrote in the middle of the story.

Hoffman coauthored *The Startup of You* with Ben Casnocha to share a philosophy: in a rapidly changing world, you should treat your career the way entrepreneurs treat startups— agile, experimental, always adapting. He could have said, "Let's wait until LinkedIn sells or until I step away. Then I'll tell my story." But he didn't.

Instead, he published while LinkedIn was still scaling. Why? Because the book wasn't just about him. It was about creating a framework leaders and professionals could use in real time. By putting the book out then, Hoffman wasn't documenting the past. He was shaping the future.

What happened next proves the point. *The Startup of You* became a bestseller, translated into multiple languages, and cemented Hoffman as more than just "the guy who started LinkedIn." The book turned him into a recognized thought leader in career strategy, leadership, and the future of work.

It gave him a platform to speak, advise, and influence far beyond the walls of LinkedIn. His book opened doors into policy discussions, global business forums, and boardrooms that might never have invited him if he was "just" a tech founder waiting for the perfect exit.

The timing mattered. By publishing while LinkedIn was still building momentum, Hoffman rode that wave and multiplied it. Readers associated his book's ideas with the platform he was scaling, and the two reinforced each other. The book positioned him, and LinkedIn, as authorities on the professional future.

Now imagine the alternative. If Hoffman had said, "I'll wait until after the company is sold," *The Startup of You* would have read like a memoir, not a playbook. It would have been looking back instead of shaping the present. Still valuable, sure, but not nearly as powerful.

By waiting, he would have missed years of being the voice in the room when people were deciding how to adapt their careers and companies. He would have missed the chance to align his personal authority with the rise of LinkedIn. He would have waited his way out of impact.

Leaders love to say they'll write *after*. After they sell the business. After they scale. After they retire. But the marketplace doesn't wait. Your competitors are writing now. They're planting their flag now. And by the time you're ready, the moment may have passed.

Reid Hoffman didn't wait until the story was over to tell it. He published while he was still living it. And that decision amplified everything else he was building.

So the real question is: **are you going to wait until your story is over, or are you going to publish now and let your book be the tool that shapes the next chapter of your leadership?**

Because **winners don't wait for "after." Winners use their book to lead in the present.**

Ben Horowitz: Why Would Anyone Care?

One of the quietest but deadliest thoughts leaders wrestle with is, "Why would anyone care about my book?" You convince yourself that your experience isn't that interesting, your lessons aren't that unique, and your market is already saturated with smarter, louder voices. But Ben Horowitz proves just how wrong that thinking is.

Today, Horowitz is known as one of Silicon Valley's most respected venture capitalists, the co-founder of Andreessen Horowitz (a16z), and a thought leader whose books have become must-reads for CEOs and entrepreneurs. But when he wrote his first book, *The Hard Thing About Hard Things* in 2014, he wasn't a celebrity in the traditional sense. He wasn't a household name outside of the tech industry. He was a former CEO who had lived through brutal realities of running a company in downturns and layoffs.

By his own admission, Horowitz wasn't trying to be the next Jim Collins or Peter Drucker. He simply asked: *What do I know that nobody else is saying?* His answer was honesty.

Most business books smooth over the messy parts. They package leadership into neat acronyms and easy-to-follow checklists. Horowitz looked at his own journey—the sleepless nights, the failed product launches, the mass layoffs, the moments when his company nearly died—and realized that the most useful thing he could offer wasn't polished formulas. It was the raw truth.

So he wrote the book he wished he'd had when he was a struggling CEO: a book about how hard leadership really is. Not how to avoid hard things, but how to deal with them when they inevitably come.

It was a risky move. Publishers could have asked, "Why would anyone care to read a book about failures, layoffs, and painful decisions?" After all, books that sell are usually about success. But Horowitz leaned into the very thing most people avoid: candor.

When *The Hard Thing About Hard Things* came out, it struck a nerve. Leaders didn't just read it—they underlined it, shared it, and kept it on their desks. Horowitz had put into words what so many CEOs were silently experiencing: that leadership often feels impossible, and that courage comes not from avoiding mistakes but from enduring them.

Your Book or Your Excuse

The book became a bestseller, recommended by everyone from Mark Zuckerberg to Sheryl Sandberg. It wasn't flashy or theoretical. It was brutally real. And that's exactly why people cared.

Here's the lesson: people care about books that tell the truth. They care about insights that feel lived-in, not polished. They care about leaders who admit, "This was hard, and here's how I survived it."

If Horowitz had said, "Why would anyone care what I have to say?" there would be no *The Hard Thing About Hard Things*. No CEOs whispering, "This book saved me." No leaders passing it down to their teams. His authority as a venture capitalist and board-level advisor grew exponentially because he was willing to put his real story out there.

When you say, "Why would anyone care about my book?" you're assuming people are looking for the most famous author, the biggest résumé, or the catchiest slogan. They're not. They're looking for honesty. They're looking for someone to show them what leadership actually feels like—not in theory, but in practice.

That's why Ben Horowitz's book worked. He didn't write as a guru with all the answers. He wrote as a leader who had been in the trenches and survived. And that was more valuable than any theory.

So let's flip the question. Instead of asking, "Why would anyone care?" ask:

❑ Who needs to hear the lessons you've already lived?

- ❑ What painful truths could you share that would save someone else years of struggle?
- ❑ How much longer will your market wait for a leader who tells it straight?

Because the reality is this: people don't care about your book because you're famous. They care about your book because it helps them.

Ben Horowitz's story proves it. The book he almost could have talked himself out of writing became the book leaders couldn't put down.

So the only real question is—are you going to hold back your lessons out of doubt, or are you going to put them in a book and let the people who need them the most finally say, "This is exactly what I needed"?

CHAPTER 22
"I Still Need to…"

What could stop you now? How's this:

"I Still Need to Do More Research"

You say you need to do more research. You need to study the publishing industry. You need to see what competitors are offering before you can make a decision. On the surface, it sounds reasonable—like you're being thorough, like you're protecting yourself from risk. But pause for a second. What exactly are you hoping to find in that research?

Let's look at who has already chosen us. The global leaders of DHL. Executives from Mitsubishi. Innovators shaping Montessori education. Do you believe these people make good decisions? Do you think they built billion-dollar companies, world-renowned brands, and life-changing educational models by being careless?

Right. So if they trusted us with their books, are you really going to uncover something they missed? Do you think your few days of internet searching will reveal a hidden truth that somehow escaped leaders who have spent entire careers making strategic choices at the highest levels?

And let's be even more direct. What exactly will your research tell you? That there are other publishers out there? Of course there are. There are always competitors in any industry. But will any amount of "shopping around" change the reality that you're here now, considering this decision, because you already know we can deliver what you need?

Think about it: when you delay to "compare options," what you're really doing is hoping that someone else can make the decision for you. You're hoping research will magically remove the risk. But there's no universe where research makes leadership risk-free. Every CEO knows this. Every founder knows this. Every leader who has ever scaled knows this. **At some point, you decide. That's why they're leaders.**

So let's ask the harder question: what happens while you're off "researching"? Time passes. Momentum fades. Competitors in your own industry move forward while you hesitate. You tell yourself you're being smart, but really, you're doing what so many leaders warn against—paralysis disguised as preparation.

And here's the irony: the more you research, the more confusion you invite. Not all research is bad—but endless research becomes noise that drowns out clarity. One publisher promises this. Another promises that. Soon you're drowning in offers and guarantees, comparing apples to oranges, and you're further away from clarity than when you started. Doesn't that sound familiar? **Research didn't bring certainty—it created noise.**

Now picture the opposite. Imagine if DHL, Mitsubishi, Montessori had said, "We'll get back to you after researching competitors." What would have happened? Nothing. No book. No impact. No legacy. They wouldn't be on shelves. They wouldn't be in readers' hands. They'd still be in "research mode." But that's not what they did, is it? They decided. They trusted their instincts and our track record. And because they acted, they're authors today—not shoppers.

So here's the choice in front of you. Do you want to be the leader who keeps circling, studying competitors, chasing an illusion of certainty? Or do you want to be the leader who recognizes that decision-making itself is the differentiator—that action, not research, is what separates the ones who write history from the ones who merely read it?

Because let's be honest: **the research you're talking about isn't research at all. It's resistance.** And the longer you indulge it, the more authority, momentum, and opportunity you lose. **You don't need more research. You need a decision**—and deep down, you already know what it is.

So tell me—when leaders at DHL, Mitsubishi, Montessori trusted us, do you believe they made good decisions? If yes, then what are you really waiting to discover? And if not—if you believe they were wrong—why would you want to follow their example in every other part of business, but not here?

The answer is clear. You don't need more research. You need a decision. And deep down, you already know which one it is.

"I Need to Sleep on It"

How many times have you said that? On the surface, it sounds thoughtful. Wise. Like you're not impulsive but measured, the kind of person who considers every angle before making a move. But let's be honest. How often is "sleeping on it" really about clarity—and how often is it simply about procrastination?

Leaders don't get where they are by waiting for inspiration to strike at three in the morning. They get there by taking action, even when it's uncomfortable. They make the call, carry the weight, and move forward. That's the pattern that created their success. So what happens when you fall back on "I'll decide tomorrow"? You shift from being an action taker to being a hesitator. From the person who moves markets to the person who hits the snooze button on their own future.

Think about the identity you're building every time you postpone. Each delay trains you to see yourself as someone who avoids decisions instead of owning them. Each "I'll decide later" erodes the muscle of decisiveness that leadership requires. What message does that send—to your team, your clients, your family? Do they see someone who seizes opportunities, or someone who stalls until the moment passes?

And let's ask the sharper question: what exactly are you going to learn overnight that you don't already know? Will a revelation appear in your dreams? Will your brain suddenly uncover data that wasn't there yesterday? Of course not. The facts are already in front of you. **What's missing isn't information—it's courage.**

Marshall Goldsmith wrote a book called *What Got You Here Won't Get You There*. The title says it all. The way you've made decisions up to this point got you to your current level. But if your next move is to keep using delay as a strategy, don't expect to breakthrough to the next stage. Because what got you here—hesitation, waiting until you feel safe, telling yourself you'll "sleep on it"—will not get you there. Leaders at the next level make decisions faster, not slower.

So be honest with yourself. If you need one more night, will anything change? Or will you simply feel the relief of avoiding the decision for another 24 hours? And if you need one more night, why not one more week? One more month? Where does that pattern end? Isn't this the very definition of procrastination—postponing what you already know you need to do, while pretending you're being responsible? Delaying decisions is like hitting snooze on your own future—you feel relief in the moment, but wake up further behind.

And what does procrastination cost you? Authority. Opportunity. Momentum. While you're "thinking," others are acting. While you're asleep, others are awake, making moves, publishing books, claiming stages, taking market share. Does that sound like the kind of leader you aspire to be—the one who waits while others win?

The truth is, the longer you delay, the more you reinforce the story that you're not a decisive person. And the more you live that story, the harder it becomes to change it. You're not just postponing a book—you're shaping your identity.

So here's the question: do you want to keep being the person who procrastinates, who hesitates, who always says, "I'll decide tomorrow"? Or do you want to be the leader who acts, who moves, who decides now?

Because every time you say, "I'll sleep on it," you're not buying clarity—you're buying comfort. And comfort is cheap. Action is priceless.

So stop pretending that tomorrow will bring something new. Tomorrow will bring the same facts you already have today. The only difference is whether you'll be the leader who took action—or the one who postponed yet again.

"I Need to Think About It"

Finally, the most common stall of all: "I need to think about it." On the surface, it sounds thoughtful. Reflective. Mature. But let's be clear—what are you really thinking about? And will that thinking actually change anything?

Steven Pressfield, in *The War of Art (2002),* gives this a name: resistance. Resistance is the invisible force that rises up whenever you move toward something important. It shows up as fear, as doubt, as hesitation, as overthinking. It whispers, "Take your time. Think it through. You're not ready yet." And here's the brutal truth: resistance never goes away. It will always show up—today, tomorrow, next week—until you take action.

So let's play this out. You say, "I need to think about it." How long will you think? A day? A week? A year? Do you really believe the fear will feel smaller the longer you sit with it? Or will it grow larger, louder, heavier, until it feels impossible to move?

What happens if you keep listening to resistance? You'll think about it forever, and action will always be "someday." But you already know someday never comes.

Now imagine the opposite. Imagine you decide now. You push through resistance instead of listening to it. Suddenly, momentum takes over. You move from thought to action, from hesitation to creation. **Resistance doesn't vanish—it just shrinks in the face of movement.**

So here's the question: will you keep thinking until the spark goes out, or will you act while the spark is alive? Will you let resistance win by stalling you into silence, or will you claim your voice by deciding?

Because the truth is this: the longer you think, the less you act. And the less you act, the more regret you stockpile. Isn't it time to stop thinking and start doing?

CHAPTER 23
The Real Excuse Behind Every Excuse

By now, you've heard every objection, and maybe you've even whispered a few of them to yourself:

- ❏ "I don't have the time."
- ❏ "It's too expensive."
- ❏ "I'm not ready yet."
- ❏ "I'm not a writer."
- ❏ "What if nobody reads it?"

Different words, same root. Because if we peel them back, every single objection leads to one place: **fear.**

Fear of wasting effort.
Fear of looking foolish.
Fear of failing.
Fear of succeeding and having to live up to it.

Here's the truth: the leaders who become authors don't wait until the fear disappears. They act *in spite of it*. They didn't mistake it for a reason to stop.

Think about the people you admire most—the ones who have books that shaped your thinking. Do you believe they never had doubts? Of course they did. The difference is that they moved forward anyway. And once their book was out in the world, the fear shrank and the opportunities multiplied.

The harsh reality is this: if you let your fear stay in charge, it won't just delay your book—it will keep you from everything your book could have created. The clients who would have found you. The stages you would have stood on. The doors would have opened. The legacy that only you can leave.

And if you're honest, deep down you already know it. Every excuse is just a mask your fear wears to sound reasonable. Strip away the disguise, and what's left is the real question:

Are you going to let fear write your story—or are you?

The moment you take action, the excuses lose their power. Fear gives way to clarity. And your book begins to take shape.

So if you've found yourself nodding along with one of these excuses, recognize it for what it is: a stall tactic. Not the truth. Not destiny. Just fear, trying to keep you safe in the comfort zone.

But safety and legacy don't live in the same neighborhood.

If you want to build something that lasts, you have to step past the excuse and into action. Because your book won't get written tomorrow, or someday, or when the stars align. It gets written when you decide it's time.

And the only honest answer left is this: **it's time.**

PART IV

Your Book, Without the Excuses

I've seen it time and again: well-intentioned leaders try to publish on their own, only to realize later that their book never really reached anyone. It's not because they didn't have something valuable to say—it's because without the right **positioning, cover, and launch strategy, even the best ideas can get lost.** A book deserves more than that.

That's why we've built a **proven process** that takes you from idea to finished product in a way that ensures your book actually gets seen, read, and acted on. It's the difference between a book that quietly sits on a shelf and one that opens doors, attracts clients, and leaves a legacy.

This process isn't for everyone. It's reserved for leaders who are ready to step into the one percent—the ones who know their ideas deserve more than a DIY effort. Not every project is a fit, and not every author is ready to lead with a book. But when it *is* the right fit, we make sure your book has every possible advantage from day one.

CHAPTER 24
Leaders Brands' Proven Process

Strategic Positioning Comes First

One of the biggest problems leaders like you face when publishing is **not knowing how to position the book for success.** That's why we always begin with a **strategy session.**

Imagine walking into a bookstore—or scrolling through one online. You want to know exactly which **bookshelf your book belongs to.** Is it entrepreneurship? Memoir? Inspirational? Motivational? Once we've identified the right shelf, we study the books that are already there. Those are your competing titles, the books your audience is reading right now.

From there, our goal is to define your **unique selling proposition (USP).** What's the reason a reader should buy *your* book instead of the others on that shelf? What's the hook that makes you stand out? This way, you enter the process with the end in mind—launching your book with the **highest possible chance of success.**

Why Positioning Matters

Before founding a publishing company, I worked one-on-one with authors. Most came to me asking for marketing help because at the time I had sold more than **80,000 copies of my own books** and wrote a book about how I did it. The problem? Their books weren't positioned correctly. Wrong title. Weak cover. Poor keywords. Off-target audience.

Sometimes we had to **rewrite the book entirely** before it could succeed. If only those authors had come to me *before* they started writing, they could have saved enormous time and money. Every one of those mistakes was fixable—but always after the fact. Our goal is to prevent them entirely. That's why we focus on strategy first.

Manuscript Development

Once we have positioning nailed down, we move to manuscript development. The first decision is: **how will the book be written?**

- ❏ Will you write it yourself?
- ❏ Do you want a book coach?
- ❏ Should we use AI to develop the manuscript from your material?
- ❏ Or do you prefer a ghostwriter?

About half of our clients choose a ghostwriter. Once your positioning is clear, I vet our writers for availability and fit, then introduce you to two. You'll meet them, review sample chapters, and decide which one to move forward with. Ghostwriting doesn't mean losing your voice—it means having a professional capture it with precision. Most of the time, clients love both chapters—and the real dilemma is choosing between them. If that happens, I'll blind-test them for you and recommend the stronger option.

Producing a 50,000-word, 200-page book typically takes **12–15 interviews, once a week** (or twice if you want to move faster). After interviews wrap, your ghostwriter usually needs about a month to deliver the manuscript.

Editing and Quality Assurance

With the manuscript complete, editing begins. We use a **combination of AI and human editors** to ensure precision, style, and polish. Multiple layers of quality assurance mean another set of human eyes always reviews your book before it goes to print.

Your book is a reflection of you. A sloppy typo can derail your credibility, so editing is never a corner we cut.

Design and Layout

Next comes interior design, formatting, and layout—where your book begins to look and feel real. This is where we turn your Word document into **a real book readers want to hold.** Standard layouts and fonts that readers love are always the baseline, but we can go custom if you prefer.

Then there's the **cover—one of the biggest success factors.** We study bestselling covers in your category, gather your preferences, and present multiple concepts. Then we refine until we land on a cover that looks good *and sells.*

As proof of how important this is: the very first edition of *Harry Potter* only sold 500 copies with its original cover design. After the cover was redesigned, it went on to become the **best-selling series in history.**

Distribution

Once your book is designed, we distribute it everywhere books are sold online. Through our partners, we also make it available to **bookstores and libraries worldwide.** This ensures your book has the same professional reach as major publishing houses.

Pre-Launch

Before your book is on sale, we secure **editorial reviews** from our wide network of successful author-clients—leaders of multinational and national companies. When new readers land on your Amazon page, even if they don't know you, they will know the names endorsing you. That **trust factor drives sales.**

We also handle **Amazon optimization,** ensuring your book shows up when people search for your topic.

Launch

With a network of over **100,000 followers and subscribers,** we're able to launch your book to bestseller status in your category. If you want the top-tier outcome, we can partner with promotional allies to hit the **top 10 on Amazon or Barnes & Noble.**

While bestseller lists create momentum, library placement creates longevity. At launch, we also notify **thousands of librarians** about your book, putting your work in the hands of readers who rely on libraries to access books. This way, your book impacts lives far beyond your immediate market.

Of course, we back this with a **comprehensive social media campaign**—creative assets, posts, shares, and reposts—to maximize reach and momentum.

Post-Launch

After launch, we invite you to our podcast, a platform that connects you directly with thousands of professionals to share your expertise and your journey as an author. This creates additional content you can use in marketing, and it expands your visibility with new audiences who may invite you onto other podcasts and speaking stages.

Finally, if your book has **international appeal,** our foreign rights agent will pitch it to publishers overseas. This creates opportunities for your book to be translated, published, and distributed in other languages—extending your influence across borders.

At the end of the day, publishing isn't about filling pages—it's about claiming your place as a leader. The 99 percent will keep making excuses, waiting for the "right time," and watching others take the opportunities they hesitated on. The one percent decide. They publish. They lead. If you're ready to join them, then this is your moment.

PART V

The Path Forward

CHAPTER 25
The Future Is Already Here

Picture this. You go to Amazon in a few years and scroll through the "new releases." The covers are professional. The titles sound smart. But when you peek inside, you can tell something's missing. They're empty. Generic. Lifeless. Because they weren't written by people at all—they were churned out by AI.

Now think about what happens when shelves, search results, and online stores are flooded with books like that. The value of a *real* book—one that carries your voice, your story, your wisdom—skyrockets.

Because here's the thing: words alone aren't valuable anymore. The internet and AI can generate billions of them at lightning speed. What *is* valuable is credibility. Authenticity. A reader's ability to trust that the person behind the book actually lived the lessons they're teaching.

That's where you come in.

Imagine your book sitting in the middle of that flood. Unlike the others, it's not just content—it's proof. Proof that you've done the work. Proof that you've earned the scars. Proof that you have a perspective no algorithm can fake. And because readers are starving for truth in a world full of manufactured words, your book doesn't just get noticed—it gets trusted.

Five years from now, when your market is asking, "Who should we follow? Who should we invest in? Who should we hire?"—they won't be fooled by a machine-written ebook. They'll look for the leaders who took the time to put their ideas into a real, lasting book.

That's why waiting isn't neutral. Waiting is dangerous. Every year you delay, more noise piles up. And every year you delay, the leaders who *do* publish are claiming the ground you could have owned.

So the real question isn't whether you should write a book. You already know the answer. The real question is: **when the shelves are full of AI-generated knockoffs, will your audience still recognize you as the real thing—if you don't?**

Your book is more than a collection of pages. It's your anchor in the storm, your proof of authority, your legacy. And in the world we're stepping into, a real book isn't just valuable. It's priceless.

The future is already here. And it's waiting for you to decide whether you'll rise above the flood—or get swept away with it.

CHAPTER 26
The Call That Changes Everything

Let me leave you with one last story.

You've met him before in these pages—the co-founder of DHL who built an empire from an idea and turned it into a legacy. When Po Chung came to me, he didn't need another accomplishment. He had already built one of the most successful service companies in history. He didn't need more credibility, more money, or more recognition. What he wanted was something bigger: to capture the philosophy and values that had carried DHL from a scrappy startup to a global powerhouse, and make sure they wouldn't be lost when he was gone.

He knew that if he didn't put his ideas into a book, someone else would tell the story—and maybe get it wrong. Or worse, it might never get told at all.

So he wrote. And because he wrote, his book *Designed to Win* didn't just sit on shelves—it shaped conversations, inspired entrepreneurs, and preserved a legacy that will outlast him by decades. Even now, after Po has passed on, his words are still teaching, guiding, and influencing leaders he'll never meet.

That's the power of a book. It travels further than you can. It speaks when you're not in the room. It tells the world not just what you did, but what you stood for.

And now it's your turn.

Your Book or Your Excuse

You've read the arguments, the examples, the stories. You know the cost of waiting. You know the difference between the 99 percent who hesitate and the one percent who act.

So the question is—are you going to let another year pass with your ideas still in your head, or are you going to take the first step toward making them permanent?

Here's what to do next: **book a call with me and my team.** We'll evaluate your book idea, test its fit for the market, and map out the exact process to bring it to life. If it's a fit, we'll help you do what Po did—turn your ideas into a book that builds authority, opens doors, and leaves a legacy.

If you've already booked your call, congratulations—you've joined the one percent. If you haven't yet, now is the moment. Because every day you wait, your competitors keep moving, and your market keeps listening to someone else's voice.

Don't let your story go untold. Don't let someone else write it for you. Decide now. **Book the call now at https://www.leadersbrands.com/appointments**. Take the path forward.

Your book or your excuse—the choice is yours.

Sources

Books and Reports Cited

Allen, Andy. *The 80 Percent Project: Unlock Exceptional Results. Live An Unimaginable Life. Create Generational Change.* United States: Leaders Press, 2024.

Chetwynd, Karen. *Led by the Child: Unlocking the Power of Montessori for All.* United Kingdom: Montessori Global Education, 2025.

Chung, Po. *Designed to Win: Strategies for Building a Thriving Global Business.* United States: Leaders Press, 2019.

Churchill, Winston. *The Second World War.* London: Cassell, 1948–1953.

Fedro, Tom. *Next Level Selling: The Definitive Guide to Closing High Dollar Deals.* United States: Leaders Press, 2019.

Ferriss, Tim. *The 4-Hour Workweek: Escape 9–5, Live Anywhere, and Join the New Rich.* New York: Harmony Books, 2007.

Goldsmith, Marshall. *What Got You Here Won't Get You There: How Successful People Become Even More Successful.* New York: Hyperion, 2007.

Grant III, Carl. *How to Live the Abundant Life.* United States: Leaders Press, 2023.

Hoffman, Reid, and Ben Casnocha. *The Startup of You: Adapt to the Future, Invest in Yourself, and Transform Your Career.* New York: Crown Business, 2012.

Horowitz, Ben. *The Hard Thing About Hard Things: Building a Business When There Are No Easy Answers.* New York: HarperBusiness, 2014.

Knight, Phil. *Shoe Dog: A Memoir by the Creator of Nike.* New York: Scribner, 2016.

Nureddine, Mark. *Pocket Mentor: The Entrepreneur's Guide to Building a Lasting Business from Scratch (Mastermind Included).* United States: Leaders Press, 2018.

Pressfield, Steven. *The War of Art: Break Through the Blocks and Win Your Inner Creative Battles.* New York: Black Irish Entertainment, 2002.

Rutkowska, Alinka. *How I Sold 80,000 Books: Book Marketing for Authors (Self Publishing through Amazon and Other Retailers).* United States: Leaders Press, 2015.

Schultz, Howard. *Onward: How Starbucks Fought for Its Life Without Losing Its Soul.* New York: Rodale Books, 2011.

Tolstoy, Leo. *War and Peace.* Moscow: The Russian Messenger, 1869.

Tufton, Christopher. *Wild Flavours: The Adventures of a Political Entrepreneur.* United States: Leaders Press, 2021.

Walt Disney Productions. *Steamboat Willie*. 1928.

Reports, Studies, and Industry References

Journal of Consumer Research. "Touch and Trust: The Power of Physical Contact in Consumer Perception." University of Chicago Press, 2017.

Journal of Management & Organization. "Leadership and Legacy: Narrative Perspectives in Organizational Continuity." Cambridge University Press, 2019.

McKinsey & Company. *The B2B Decision-Making Journey.* McKinsey & Company, 2023.

Yale University. "A Chapter a Day: Association Between Book Reading and Longevity." *Social Science & Medicine,* 2016.

Web and Reference Sources

Carter, Allison. "Edelman and LinkedIn Report: The True Impact of B2B Thought Leadership." *Ragan Communications*, March 4, 2024.
https://www.ragan.com/edelman-and-linkedin-report-thought-leadership/

Edelman and LinkedIn. "2024 Edelman–LinkedIn B2B Thought Leadership Impact Report." *Edelman*, 2024. https://www.edelman.com/expertise/Business-Marketing/2024-b2b-thought-leadership-report

Miller, Donald. "StoryBrand Your Business Live." *StoryBrand*. https://storybrand.com/live/

Olajide, David. "The Impact of Thought Leadership: Edelman and LinkedIn B2B 2024 Report." *The PR Insider by Curzon PR*, July 22, 2024. https://curzonpr.com/theprinsider/the-impact-of-thought-leadership-edelman-and-linkedin-b2b-2024-report

The Black Swan Group. "Never Split The Difference: Negotiating As If Your Life Depended On It." https://www.blackswanltd.com/never-split-the-difference

Wikipedia. "Alexander Haslam." https://en.wikipedia.org/wiki/Alexander_Haslam

Media and Public Domain References

Churchill, Winston S. "Nobel Prize in Literature, 1953." *NobelPrize.org.*
https://www.nobelprize.org/prizes/literature/1953/churchill

Gates, Bill. "Best Books of 2016: *Shoe Dog.*" *Gates Notes,* 2016. https://www.gatesnotes.com/Books/Shoe-Dog

Grant, Adam. "The Surprising Habits of Original Thinkers." *TED,* 2016. https://www.ted.com/talks/adam_grant_the_surprising_habits_of_original_thinkersa

The New York Times. "Cal Newport on Deep Work." *The New York Times,* 2016.

The Economist. "Eric Ries and The Lean Startup." *The Economist,* 2011.